This book belongs to:

_____

The
PRAIRIE TABLE

Suppers, Potlucks & Socials—
Crowd-Pleasing Recipes to Bring People Together

✦✦✦✦✦✦✦✦✦✦

Karlynn Johnston

appetite
by RANDOM HOUSE

Appetite by Random House® and colophon are registered trademarks of
Penguin Random House LLC.

Library and Archives of Canada Cataloguing in Publication is available upon request.

ISBN: 978-0-14-753110-0

eBook ISBN: 978-0-14-753111-7

Cover and book design by Leah Springate

Interior images: (linen background) © Sally Williams Photography, (linen napkin) © didecs, both
Getty Images; (various borders) freevector.com and vecteezy.com

Printed and bound in China

Published in Canada by Appetite by Random House® a division of Penguin Random House LLC.

www.penguinrandomhouse.ca

10 9 8 7 6 5 4 3 2 1

This book is dedicated to all of you that read, support, and enjoy the Kitchen Magpie website. Without our almost decade-long online love affair, none of this would have happened.

CONTENTS

Welcome to My Prairie Table!

L iving in the Prairies is all about socializing, spending time with those we love, and enjoying tasty food. The last meal of the day has always been the most important. Breakfast is often toast in the car when my kids are running late for school. Our family eats lunches at school with friends or outside the home with clients. Even farmers are up and out the door before the sun, and lunch is often a packed sandwich eaten out in the field. But supper? Supper is together at the table. Supper is almost always at home, with everyone congregating together for perhaps the first time that day. This need to reconnect at the end of the day with the act of breaking bread at a table together is still just as important today, for farm and city folk alike, as it was in the past.

When prioritizing schedules in our busy lives, we also place great importance on parties and get-togethers in our free time. Perhaps it's because not so long ago the bleakness of isolation was very real (and still can be in rural farming areas on the Prairies) and connecting with others in your community was always of the utmost importance. My Grandma Kay lived out in Pine River, Manitoba, a very small community where there was the church, the graveyard, the school, and the community hall. The community hall was a couple of miles from their homestead, yet every Friday night, the local girls would put on their best dresses and stockings and head to the dance. Sometimes they could take the wagon, but most times they would have to walk. And walk they did, even in the winter in those stockings and dresses, because other than church on Sundays, that Friday night social was the only time during the week to enjoy time visiting with members of the community.

Just the word "socials" alone evokes memories of days gone by when the main form of entertainment was getting together with friends and family for eating, drinking, and visiting with each other at events like barn raisings, church picnics, and harvest dinners. Even today, whether it's two people having coffee and dainties, your family sitting down at the table for a nice Sunday dinner, or a big potluck or picnic, the thread connecting all these gatherings is the serving of food we love.

The recipes you will find in this book are what we eat as a family, what we feed our guests at our home, and what we take to gatherings. Whether a salad or vegetable dish, home-baked buns or easy main meal, every recipe in this book is easily cut in half for a smaller family meal or doubled for a large event—even the cocktails (though why you'd want to cut cocktails in half escapes me). I also wanted every recipe in this book to be useful week in and week out, to make your life easier.

You can make a full batch of a crowd-pleasing recipe to take to a soiree or to feed your own guests, whether a side dish or a main course. There are kid-friendly recipes for dinners that will also be perfect for potlucks. There are easy dinner recipes such as Slow-Cooker Beef Dips on page 154 that also make perfect leftovers that the entire family can eat for lunch the next day, or freeze them for a later date. My Calico Beans on page 156 might be a go-to potluck dish, but my family eats it twice a month and the kids take it in thermoses for lunches. The salads and vegetable dishes are all sides that you can make any day of the week. The dainties section is perfect for filling up your freezer, to pull out for surprise visitors (so that you have something to serve with coffee!) or the holiday season. There's nothing like a tray of dainties to get Prairie folks at a party excited!

You're going to see classics (such as Marion's perogies (see page 17), which I make in triple batches so I only have to make them once every couple of months) and some fresh new favorites (like the Garlic and Brown Sugar Bacon Pineapple Bites on page 103 that will make you want to throw a tiki-themed party just so that you can serve them).

I'm also bringing my husband, Mike, aka Mr. Kitchen Magpie, into the cookbook fray. He's in charge of cocktails in our house and, due to popular demand, he now even has his own section on the Kitchen Magpie website, where he creates cocktails for everyone to enjoy. I heard from a lot (and I mean a LOT!) of you after my first book that I needed to do more cocktails, so there's an entire chapter of his cocktails and mocktails at the end of this book just for you.

This is us. This how we eat, this is how I cook for those I love, and, if you will indulge me, this is an entire cookbook's worth of recipes from my table to yours. I'm so very happy to share these recipes with you.

Love,
Karlynn

Russian Cucumber Lemonade (page 242)

Big Ukrainian Party on the Prairie

I once had a relative regale me with stories about how she went for coffee at an acquaintance's house and said acquaintance served coffee . . . with nothing to eat. I still laugh when I think about her utter incredulity over how there was nothing served with the coffee. You'd have to be part of a family like mine to understand how this was just the craziest thing a hostess could do, I suppose, but in my family as soon as you set foot in the house as a guest you are immediately offered food and drink. We just have this crazy need to feed people.

My family gatherings are loud, boisterous, and always eventful, and they're full of food and *definitely* lots to drink (we are Ukrainian, after all) no matter whether the event celebrates new life, the joining of two lives in marriage, the end of a life well lived, or simply the joy of living, eating, and being with each other.

As with any culture, our food customs are weaved intricately into our gatherings, even somber ones. If you are from a family of Ukrainian descent, you may recognize the word *provody* (and if not, you will most likely have experienced its influence). Provody, also known as the Blessing of the Graves, is a Ukrainian remembrance festivity or memorial service for the deceased, very similar to the Day of the Dead but taking place in the spring, usually the Monday or Tuesday after Easter Sunday. Food and drink are eaten at the ancestral gravesites, with some being left for the deceased to put their spirits at ease so that they may continue to rest in peace in the afterlife, and it has since evolved into our own modern version of a centuries-old tradition. When my Grandma Kay was laid to rest in a small, remote rural Manitoba graveyard along with her parents, miles and miles from any town, my uncle had made sure to bring a trunkful of wine and kielbasa for after the ceremony. What I am trying to convey is just how important food and gatherings are for all of us no matter the occasion, and not just to those of us with Eastern European ancestry. No matter what the event, the first thing my mom will ask is "What are we feeding everyone?"

This book begins with the recipes that we make for our family gatherings. The dishes are mainly Ukrainian, but you'll notice that many have Polish and Russian influences. These are some of our most beloved traditional recipes, and when we take the quite considerable amount of time and effort to make them, it's always for an occasion with loved ones. It's because our hearts fill with happiness knowing that everyone at the table will be thinking of Grandma Kay while eating her perogies (see page 16), or that serving the nalysnyky (see page 27) will inevitably get everyone talking about their own variations.

As you read through, I want you to look for ways that your own family incorporates bits and pieces from your culture into modern-day parties, gatherings, and yes, even funerals. How toasts are made to loved ones who are no longer with us, how all the amazing phases of life are celebrated in so many ways, on different days, in so many diverse cultures—and how almost all of it incorporates food and drink. Maybe you too throw wild, crazy get-togethers where your uncle has too much wine and starts telling dirty jokes. Or you argue good-naturedly over how to make perogies or the best holop-chi (see page 29) and then tease your cousin about how she likes to eat perogies with jam (I still don't really get it).

What I do know, my darlings, is when I'm gone, please bring some of my Grandma Marion's perogies and a nice glass of red wine to my grave for a little visit. And maybe a Coffee Crisp or two.

Little Cheater on the Prairie

If you have a copy of my first cookbook, *Flapper Pie and a Blue Prairie Sky*, you will have read how I can't give up certain things that should have my cookbook author card revoked. I love instant pistachio pudding mix. I adore canned cream of mushroom soup and will never give it up. Canned smoked oysters are my weakness. Packaged liverwurst and I meet every Christmas with a box of vegetable crackers, and I call it "dinner." I need a monthly fix of a certain fast-food Filet-O-Fish sandwich—the admission of which should definitely have sent you all running by now. The list is endless.

But you haven't run away, so I guess you are just taking me and my food foibles as a package deal.

It's a mental challenge as a cookbook author to create recipes using prepackaged goods because you feel that you should only be including the fanciest, most extravagant recipes for the people who are buying your cookbook with their hard-earned money. Then I remember that there are days when I lose the keys to my car in the house, the kids forgot to tell me about swim practice times being moved, Mike's out of town for a client, and I promised to bring dessert for brunch with friends tomorrow morning. Remember my motto, "It's all about balance."

So when life rains lemons, make lemonade, add some bourbon to it, and whip up one of my cheater recipes to save your sanity. These cheater recipes are seriously the best recipes I make that use packaged and canned goods. There are only a few scattered throughout the book. To find them you'll see a little "cheater recipe" logo in the top of the recipe page. This will let you know that it's a fun, fast, and delicious recipe that cuts corners when it counts. When you are in a hurry or are short on time, look for that symbol to help you out!

Trust me, my dears: when you have spent the entire day making some of the Ukrainian recipes in Chapter 1 and are neck-deep in perogy dough, you are going to be eternally grateful that I gave you the easiest recipe for Pistachio Pudding Cookies, page 187—which are my very favorite cookie ever. It's all about balance!

Have fun looking for the cheater recipes and enjoy them, as you should!

—"Cheater Cheater Pistachio Pudding Cookie Eater" Karlynn

Brief Pantry Notes

There are a few ingredients in this cookbook where I am very specific about what to use, and it is always for a taste or a texture reason. To clarify, I thought I'd add some small notes here to lessen any confusion.

INGREDIENT SIZING

It is a well-known and frustrating fact that canned goods and prepackaged items are measured differently in Canada than they are in the US. For example, our pudding mixes are 99 grams, while in the States they are 96 grams. We don't all have the same sizes of canned pineapple, canned condensed milk . . . the list goes on and on. Use sizes as close as you can get to what I have in the recipes.

SALT

Unless I specify sea salt, regular table salt is to be used. I used sea salt when I feel that the dish benefits from having a salty crunch to it, such as my Dill Monkey Bread on page 72. Sprinkling table salt on top of bread just isn't the same.

BUTTER

Unless specified, use unsalted butter. There are instances where I ask for salted—for example, in sweet icing glazes where the added salt makes a perfect foil for the sweetness. Those who bought my first book will know my love of using salted butter!

SASKATOON BERRIES

Speaking of my first cookbook, that sweet Prairie berry is very common in my cooking in this book again. Saskatoons, also known as serviceberries, ripen on their large, bushy trees by the beginning of July. The plump purple berries freeze exceptionally well. Simply flash-freeze them on baking sheets, and then transfer to large freezer-safe bags to store. They can be frozen for six to eight months. You can buy them at local farmers' markets in the Canadian Prairie provinces during the summer and freeze a stash of them for winter baking and cooking. If you don't have these berries in your area, you can substitute blueberries in any and all recipes in this book.

Chapter One

UKRAINIAN DISHES

COOKING THESE HERITAGE RECIPES

My mom was an invaluable source of information and a huge help for this chapter, but she fretted about the nature of the recipes during the entire process of testing and putting together the material with me. You wouldn't think that a chapter full of my heritage recipes would bring forth such a fuss, but bringing recipes to you that my family has made from old notes and half-written instructions was a feat and a half. We worked from faded notes, bad photocopies, and instructions that only a member of our family could decipher.

Yet here they are, developed into working recipes for you all to enjoy thanks to endless hours of work from me and (mainly) my mom, who understood the processes that my grandmas and babas (my great-grandmas) were using better than I ever could. Also, asking my mom to come up with precise measurements for recipes that she has cooked by sight, taste, and feel for decades was a big thing to ask!

While they do have measurements now, these recipes lend themselves to their various components not matching up with each other, and the actual recipe yields are very fluid. How can I tell you the exact size of cabbage leaf to use in your cabbage rolls? I can't. I could send you with a measuring tape to the grocery store to buy precisely the right size of cabbage, and you'd open it to find you have crazy-sized leaves inside. Recipes were, and still are, made with what nature provides and what you have on hand. Even the potatoes in perogies are completely different to work with, depending on the season. My Grandma Kay would never make perogies in the summer because of the quality of potatoes. Instead, she would wait for the potato season to start anew so she'd have fresh potatoes to make the best perogies, or she used stored ones from the previous year's harvest.

My mom is the only person I know who can come close to matching up perogy dough to filling, but that's thanks to decades of rolling dough to the precise thickness. She just *knows*. If you roll that perogy dough slightly too thick, you'll be left with extra filling. Slightly thinner, and you won't have enough filling. Mine never match up—I'm just going to come out and say that right now. The good news is that almost everything in these recipes freezes well for your next batch, but that perogy filling? We basically just eat it as a snack if any is left over. And you can't go wrong: it's cheesy mashed potatoes, after all.

Tackle the recipes in this chapter with the intent of learning the process for yourself and finding your rhythm. When you're making heritage recipes like this is the only time in my cookbook writing career that I am going to tell you these following recipe truths:

- The yields I have written in the next chapter will almost certainly be different for you than they are for me.
- You are most likely going to have leftover dough when you make perogies, until you find your method.
- You might run out of filling for cabbage rolls or have to crack open some more tomato soup because you like it with more sauce.

I promised my mom that I would warn you, so warn you I have. This advice is most applicable to the first three recipes here: the entire Choose Your Own Perogy Adventure section, nalysnyky and holopchi. The others were easier to replicate into a "real" recipe format for you all.

Now before you start, to keep with Ukrainian tradition at the table, before anyone eats, raise your glasses (coffee, whiskey, anything will do) in a toast with me and say "Dai bozhe zdorov'ya!" (May God give you health!).

Now, onward to perogy pinching!

Choose Your Own Perogy Adventure

No matter how you spell it, the humble perogy/perogie/pyrohy/pierogi is one of the most beloved Eastern European dishes and probably the best known. This recipe is one that many family friends have been waiting for: my Grandma Marion's secret perogy recipe. The only people who have had this recipe were Baba, Grandma, and then Mom. And yes, she spelled it "perogy"; it's in her handwriting on her recipe. Everyone always argues with me, but you know what? She spoke fluent Ukrainian and made the BEST perogies on the Prairies, so she could spell it however she wanted!

My mom is now the flagbearer for making the best perogies, and everyone, from my high school friends to my siblings and kids, have devoured them for every occasion. She has carried on as the perogy maker and regularly fills my freezer so that my kids can cook them and take them to school in their thermoses for lunch. My mom made hundreds upon hundreds of these perogies for the caterer to serve at my sister's and my weddings, because not having the family perogies at our big Ukrainian weddings was utterly unthinkable—and the thought of handing over the recipe to a stranger to make our family recipe was worth a collective chuckle. Yet here we are, happily and excitedly handing over our cherished recipe to all of you—and I'll give Mom credit; she must have seen the food writer in me and just simply waited until she could get the recipe published for all to enjoy Grandma's perogy legacy. When I told one of my best friends from high school that my mom was finally releasing the family recipe, she said—and I quote her directly—"It's about damn time!"

This is a fairly complex recipe, and I suggest that beginners start with the Polish Perogies (page 16) to get a feel for working with the dough. This recipe should feel like a soft, velvety dough that rests gently in the bowl when you have the right amount of flour. My mom remembers my baba standing in the kitchen talking to everyone, bowl on her hip, working the flour into the dough with her fingertips, not even looking at it. She knew by touch when the dough was ready, and with practice, so you will you.

✦ ✦ ✦

Time Warning

Perogies are an all-day venture. Make sure that you allow yourself a lot of time to make these. We don't freeze the perogy dough, as my mom swears that it loses its velvety texture and isn't as nice to work with, so be ready for a few hours of work after you prep the dough.

✦ ✦ ✦

see over

Grandma Kay's Polish Pierogi Dough

Grandma Kay had a lot of pierogi recipes tucked away in her recipe collection—with her main peroghys recipe so complex that no one in my family has even mastered it yet! You'll note that her spelling of the word is different for both recipes and perhaps it's because this is a Polish version. She used two different spellings in her recipes. I found this recipe written onto a blank notes page in one of her favorite community church cookbooks, obviously a place where she wrote down her recipes to keep for later. I'm not sure why she called them "Polish perogies" or what actually makes them Polish, but that is the name she wrote down. This is the perfect recipe for beginners; it relies less on learning how the dough should feel than Marion's Perogy Dough recipe on the next page does, and you can get a feel for working with the dough before you try a more difficult recipe.

Makes enough dough for 7–8 dozen perogies |
Prep Time: 2 hours | Total Time: 2 hours, 15 minutes

½ cup butter, melted and cooled slightly

2 eggs, beaten well

1¼ cups water

3 Tbsp sour cream

1 tsp salt

6 cups all-purpose flour

1. Combine the butter, eggs, water, and sour cream in a large mixing bowl.
2. Whisk the salt and flour together, then add to the wet mixture. Mix together until a soft, velvety dough forms, adding a bit more flour if needed. The dough will be slightly sticky, but you should be able to shake it off your hands easily.
3. Let the dough rest for 30 minutes.
4. Select your filling recipe from pages 18–20 and prepare.
5. Next, turn to the Perogy Dough Rolling Instructions and Perogy Filling and Pinching Instructions on pages 20 and 23 respectively.

Marion's Perogy Dough

Here it is, the secret recipe finally revealed! Now everyone can know that the hidden ingredient in Grandma Marion's perogy recipe is instant potato flakes in the dough. Yes, the instant potato flakes aren't for the filling, but for using in the actual dough itself, which was brilliant of her. Not only do the flakes add a great potato flavor to the dough, the extra potato starch contributes to the luxurious velvety texture of the dough. These perogies are well worth the amount of time they take to make. So without further ado, my family's secret perogy recipe.

Makes enough dough for 7–8 dozen perogies | Prep Time: 15 minutes |
Total Time: 3 hours, 15 minutes, including resting

½ cup butter, cubed

1 cup boiling water

1½ cups cold water

¾ cup instant potato flakes

¼ tsp salt

5 cups all-purpose flour, more if needed

Additional flour for rolling

1. Place the butter in a large mixing bowl. Pour the cup of boiling water over it and stir until the butter is completely melted. Add the cold water and stir to combine. Mix in the potato flakes and salt until dissolved.

2. Mix in the flour until a soft, velvety dough forms. The dough will be slightly sticky, but you should be able to shake it off your hands easily. Add more flour, if necessary.

3. Cover the bowl with plastic wrap, then drape a clean, dry tea towel over top and let rest in a warm, draft-free spot for 90 minutes.

4. Select your filling recipe from pages 18–20 and prepare.

5. Next, skip ahead to the Perogy Dough Rolling Instructions and Perogy Filling and Pinching Instructions on pages 20 and 23 respectively.

Perogy Fillings

These fillings will generally yield enough filling for seven to eight dozen perogies using the two perogy dough recipes on pages 16–17, but remember, it all depends on how many dough circles you roll out and how much filling you use—or how much you sneak on the side. I'm totally guilty of snacking on hot cheesy potato filling. You can use any of these fillings in either dough recipe with remarkable success. The fillings can be made ahead of time and stored in the refrigerate for a day or two, or frozen and then defrosted when you are ready to use them. Please note that all of the prep and cook times are only for the fillings and do not include dough time or perogy filling and pinching time.

CHEESE POTATO FILLING (GRANDMA MARION'S AND MOM'S FAMOUS FILLING)

When most people think of a traditional perogy, it's almost always the cheese filling type that comes to mind first. It is the most simple of all perogy fillings to make, with the trick being to use an excellent sharp-tasting old cheese that has a ton of flavor. With all of this work that you have already put into making the dough, don't skimp on the cheese for the filling!

Makes 4–5 cups filling | Prep Time: 15 minutes | Total Time: 30 minutes

4 lb russet potatoes, peeled then sliced into 1-inch-thick pieces

2 cups shredded old cheddar cheese

Salt and pepper

1. In a large stockpot full of cold, unsalted water over medium-high heat, boil the potatoes until just done, about 15 minutes. They should be soft enough for a fork to pierce through, yet not fall apart. Drain well and return to the pot.
2. Add the cheese and mash the potatoes until smooth and lump-free. Add salt and pepper to taste. Let the filling cool completely before using.

✦ ✦ ✦

Mom's Potato Tips

1. Peel your potatoes as thinly as possible, as you are measuring by weight, not volume. Make sure you get as much potato as you can. I learned this thanks to many scoldings over the years regarding my too-thick potato peels.

2. Boil the potatoes until they are just fork-tender and can be mashed. Boiling the potatoes too long will add moisture to the filling that isn't needed or wanted.

✦ ✦ ✦

SASKATOON BERRY FILLING

Saskatoon berries grow abundantly on the Canadian Prairies, and these perogies are the very definition of working with what nature provides you. You won't find these perogies anywhere except where saskatoon berries grow, making them a regional tradition that is to be treasured. You may use blueberries instead if you don't have saskatoons where you live, and they are exceptional as well!

5–6 dozen perogies | Prep Time: 3 minutes | Total Time: 3 minutes

3–4 cups saskatoon berries, fresh or frozen (thaw frozen berries on paper towels)

1 cup white sugar

1. For each saskatoon perogy, place 4 to 5 berries in the center of the circle of dough (or 2 to 3 if the berries are large).
2. Sprinkle with ¼ teaspoon of sugar and proceed with the rest of the perogy-pinching instructions.
3. Eat these perogies with heavy cream and a sprinkle of sugar in a bowl after cooking.

PRUNE FILLING

Ukrainians love their prune fillings—you'll often find it in perishke and rolled breads—so it's no surprise that we also make perogies that are filled with prunes. We don't make a full batch of these as they are a dessert perogy and not to everyone's taste; instead we pair them with another fruit-filled perogy to use up the batch of perogy dough. This recipe will yield enough filling for 2 to 3 dozen perogies.

Makes 1½–2 cups filling | Prep Time: 5 minutes | Total Time: 25 minutes

2 cups pitted and diced prunes

1 cup warm water

½ cup white sugar

2 tsp lemon juice

⅛ tsp ground cinnamon

⅛ tsp ground cloves

Pinch of salt

1. In a medium-sized stockpot, bring the prunes, water, and sugar to a boil over medium-high heat.
2. Mix in the lemon juice, cinnamon, cloves, and salt. Bring to a low boil over medium-high heat and boil gently for 15 to 20 minutes, until the mixture has thickened, stirring occasionally to prevent it from burning.
3. Remove from the heat and let cool completely before using. This will fill 2 to 3 dozen perogies. I suggest making these and more fruit-filled perogies to use up all your dough.

SAUERKRAUT BACON FILLING

You will most likely have leftovers to snack on with this filling thanks to sauerkraut usually being canned in 1-quart jars. Just fry up the entire jar for the recipe below and eat whatever is left with a poached egg on top. It will change your world.

Makes 4–5 cups filling | Prep Time: 10 minutes | Total Time: 25 minutes

1-quart (32-oz) jar of sauerkraut
2 Tbsp salted butter
6 strips of bacon, diced very small
1 cup finely diced yellow onion
Salt and pepper

1. Drain the sauerkraut thoroughly. Melt the butter in a frying pan over medium-high heat, then add the sauerkraut. Fry for 10 to 15 minutes, until softened and all the remaining liquid has evaporated. Scoop into a bowl and set aside.
2. Add the bacon and onion to the frying pan and sauté for about 15 minutes, until the onions are soft and translucent and the bacon has shrunk and released a lot of its grease. Drain the grease. Add the sauerkraut and fry for another 10 minutes, stirring constantly, until the entire mixture is soft. Add salt and pepper to taste.
3. Cool completely before using.

CREATING THE RECIPES

Perogy Dough Rolling Instructions

1. Lightly flour your work surface. Divide the dough into 3 evenly sized portions for easier rolling. Keep unused portions covered, but not refrigerated. The dough will lose its velvety texture if you place it in the fridge, so plan to make all of the perogies in a day.
2. Roll the dough out on the floured surface to ⅛-inch thickness. Take a 2½-inch cookie cutter (we use a clean empty soup can!) and cut as many circles as you can out of the dough. Gather the dough, roll it out again, and cut more circles, repeating the process until all the dough is used from the first portion of dough. The magic of Grandma's dough is that it can be rerolled many times without losing its consistency; just remember to keep it at room temperature or it will get tougher.
3. Follow step 1 of the Perogy Filling and Pinching Instructions (page 23).
4. Repeat with the second and then third portions of dough.

Perogy Filling and Pinching Instructions

1. Allow yourself a good 45–60 minutes to fill and pinch your perogies.
2. To fill the perogies, take a heaping teaspoon of filling and place it in the center of the dough circle. Fold over the dough into a half-circle shape and pinch the edges together well. Mom will pinch the edges 3 to 4 times on each perogy to make sure they are closed. We do not dampen the edges of the perogies as it decreases the dough quality; we just pinch the edges together multiple times. Take your time on each one, and they won't fall apart.
3. You can cook the perogies right away (see cooking instructions below) or freeze them for later.

Freezing Perogies

All of the perogy recipes in this cookbook can be frozen. While you can freeze the fillings to use later, you don't want to freeze the dough separately as you will lose that velvety texture. You will only want to freeze rolled, cut, and filled perogies.

1. To freeze perogies, place them on parchment-lined cookie sheets and put them, uncovered, in the freezer for about 2 hours.
2. When they're completely frozen, transfer them to large, good-quality freezer-safe plastic bags and keep frozen for later use.
3. You can freeze perogies for up to 6 months, but I doubt they'll last that long before you eat them!

Perogy Cooking Instructions

This method is for cooking the perogies from fresh or frozen. Do NOT defrost the frozen perogies before cooking.

1. Bring a large stockpot of water to a boil over high heat.
2. Place 2 to 3 dozen perogies in the water, stirring to ensure they don't stick to the bottom. Once they start to float, cook them for another 2 to 3 minutes. It's a complete myth that perogies are done as soon as they float—unless you want raw dough! Cook them until the dough puffs up slightly and loses the raw-dough look.
3. Remove the perogies, drain, and toss with butter to prevent them from sticking to one another. If desired, you can also fry the perogies at this point. If not, serve the perogies immediately.
4. To fry, place 2 to 3 tablespoons of butter in a large skillet. Melt the butter over medium-high heat and then add the perogies. Fry for 5 to 6 minutes on each side, until they are crispy and brown. Remove and serve immediately.
5. Serve topped with sour cream, more butter, fried onions, bacon, gravy, or even jam!

Ukrainian Onion, Cream, and Dill Sauce

We Ukrainians put this stuff on *everything*. This is our go-to sauce that we pour over whatever Baba cooks up. New potatoes? Check. Perishke? You betcha. Frog's legs? This sauce is a must! (You'll have to check out the Frog's Legs recipe on page 37 to see what I'm talking about, but let me assure you that no frogs were hurt in the making of this book.) Feel free to use this on anything you can think of!

Makes 3–4 cups sauce | Prep Time: 10 minutes | Total Time: 30 minutes

2 Tbsp salted butter

2 cups finely diced white onion

½ cup fresh dill, chopped
  (or 3 Tbsp dried dill)

3 cups heavy cream

Salt

1. Melt the butter in a large skillet over medium-high heat. Add the onions and fry until very soft, about 15 minutes. Mix in the dill and fry for another 1 to 2 minutes.

2. Turn down the heat to medium-low, pour in the cream, and stir until combined. Simmer for 2 to 3 minutes, stirring constantly. The cream will reduce slightly. You can cook it longer and reduce the liquid down for a thicker sauce if desired. Once done, add the salt to taste.

3. Pour over desired dish and enjoy.

4. The sauce can be refrigerated in an airtight container for up to 2 days, but is best served right away as it can separate.

Nalysnyky (Ukrainian Crepes)

This might be my favorite Ukrainian dish of all, even over perogies. These crepes are filled with a rich, dill-icious cottage/ricotta cheese filling that is out of this world, and not only that, they are baked up together layered with butter when it's time to serve them. One person does the crepes, one person does the filling, and then we wrap them and freeze them individually on baking sheets. When wrapped in freezer bags or containers, nalysnyky freeze exceptionally well for a couple of months—if they last that long! These also tend to taste better when cooked from frozen as the fresh crepes tend to fall apart, so this is a great make-ahead meal. We usually make a few batches in 1 day to stock up.

Use a 7-inch skillet or actual crepe pan of similar size, as making the crepes becomes far easier and they turn out the perfect size—and a pan that size is also great for omelets.

Makes 2–2½ dozen crepes | Prep Time: 40 minutes |
Total Time: 2 hours, 40 minutes

Crepes

2 eggs

1¼ cups milk

2 Tbsp canola oil

½ tsp salt

1 cup flour

Filling

2 cups dry cottage cheese curd

¾ cup ricotta cheese
   (10% milk fat)

2 egg yolks

2 Tbsp whipping cream

1 tsp dill or 1 Tbsp fresh dill if in
   season

1 tsp salt

Salted butter for topping when
   cooking

1. To make the crepes, whisk together the eggs, milk, oil, and salt in a medium-sized bowl. Add the flour in small batches, whisking the batter until smooth after each pour, until it is all incorporated.

2. Lightly oil a 7-inch skillet, then heat over medium-high heat.

3. Pour in about 3 tablespoons of batter into the skillet, tilting the pan to swirl the batter until it covers the entire bottom of the pan in a thin film. Cook for 30 to 40 seconds, until the bottom is lightly browned and the edges lift easily. Flip the crepe, then cook the other side for another 30 to 40 seconds, until the center of the crepe is cooked and set.

4. Transfer each cooked crepe to wire racks to cool individually. Do not stack or they will stick. Do not use waxed paper either.

5. In a medium-sized bowl, add the cottage cheese curd, ricotta cheese, egg yolks, whipping cream, dill, and salt. Using a fork, mix until combined.

see over

6. To fill the crepes, place 2 to 3 tablespoons of filling in the center of each one, making a small mound that is a ½ inch shorter than the crepe at each end as you don't want the filling to squish out the ends of the roll. Starting at one long side of the filling, roll the crepe over the filling like a carpet roll, then place the crepe seam side down onto a parchment-lined baking sheet. Repeat until you run out of crepes or filling.

7. To freeze for later, place the baking sheet in the freezer for 1 to 2 hours until frozen solid, and then transfer to freezer-safe containers or bags. These can be frozen for up to 3 months.

8. To cook from fresh or frozen, fit the desired number of nalysnyky in an appropriately sized greased casserole dish in 2 or 3 layers, dabbing pieces of salted butter randomly on top of a few crepes in each row. You can cook anywhere from 12 of these in a small casserole to 36 of them in a large roaster—or more. Just keep them in 2 or 3 layers. Cover with a lid or a sheet of aluminum foil and cook in a 350°F oven for 45 to 60 minutes or until they reach 165°F in the middle. Serve hot.

✦ ✦ ✦

We usually have crepes left over. You can eat them with scrambled eggs in them or, you know, whipped cream and chocolate sauce.

✦ ✦ ✦

Holopchi (Ukrainian Cabbage Rolls)

When it comes to ingredients, nothing (except, perhaps, perogies) is as personalized as the cabbage roll. Some people use beef, others use pork, or bacon, or no meat at all. Some recipes use tomato juice, others use a favorite canned tomato soup. I've seen dill, garlic, and more added to these; it's pretty much up to you what you want to fill them with. This is how both of my grandmas made them, and it's how my family still makes them today. I prefer the more complex taste of a favorite tomato soup than plain tomato juice. Feel free to add more sauce at the end; my dad likes his cabbage rolls quite dry, while I love mine swimming in soup. The choice is up to you! This recipe calls for medium-grain rice, which is exactly what my grandma used. She would hunt down Calrose rice, which is the rice that started the California rice industry! Today, you can usually find medium-grain rice in the specialty sections of grocery stores. If not, short-grain rice will work just as well.

Our no-boil method for the cabbage is a handy trick: core it and freeze it in a plastic bag the night before and thaw it in the morning. You don't have to boil the cabbage because the freezing process helps the leaves come apart more easily.

Makes 3–4 dozen cabbage rolls | Prep Time: 1 hour |
Total Time: 3 hours, 30 minutes to 4 hours

2 cups medium- or short-grain rice, uncooked

1 Tbsp butter

½ cup finely diced white onion

½ lb ground beef

½ lb ground pork

2–3 cans (10½ oz/284 mL each) your favorite condensed tomato soup or 2½ cups tomato juice

1 tsp salt

½ tsp pepper

1 large green cabbage, core removed, frozen in a plastic bag overnight, then thawed in the morning

1. Rinse the rice thoroughly, then cook according to package directions, taking 3 minutes off the cooking time. The rice should be slightly underdone. Drain the rice and rinse with cold water to stop the cooking process, then drain again completely. Transfer to a large bowl.

2. In a large frying pan over medium-high heat, melt the butter and fry the onion until it's soft and translucent, around 15 minutes. Add the ground beef and pork and fry until no longer pink. Drain off the grease and let the meat cool in the pan.

3. Once cool enough to touch, transfer the meat and onions to the large bowl and combine gently with the rice.

4. Pour a ½ cup of the condensed soup or juice into the rice mixture, and add the salt and pepper. Mix the meat, soup, and rice together gently until combined. Set the filling aside.

5. Unfurl the cabbage leaves, using the most tender medium-sized leaves first.

see over

6. Spoon about 3 tablespoons of filling onto each leaf, depending on the leaf size. Roll the cabbage leaf around the filling, then tuck the ends in toward the middle of the roll. Most recipes don't tuck the ends, but we've found that if you push them in after rolling, more often than not they stay tucked in.

7. Preheat the oven to 350°F.

8. Place some cabbage trimmings in the bottom of a large greased roasting pan that has a lid. Place 2 dozen cabbage rolls seam side down onto the trimmings.

9. Dilute the soup in the opened can with an equal amount of water, and prepare the second can of soup with the required amount of water (see the can directions). If you are using tomato juice, use 3 cups of juice. Pour a third of the soup or juice over the first layer. Place another layer on top of the first, then top with half of the remaining soup. Repeat for a third layer and top with the last of the soup. If you like more sauce, you can mix a third can of soup with water and pour it over.

10. Place the lid on the pan and cook for 2½ to 3 hours, until the cabbage leaves are tender. Remove and serve hot.

✦ ✦ ✦

If you don't want to cook the cabbage rolls immediately, you can freeze them. You do not want to freeze already cooked rolls, as they can be too soft after reheating. To freeze, place each cabbage roll seam side down on parchment-lined baking sheets. Freeze completely, then transfer to a freezer-safe plastic bag or container and store for up to 3 months. To cook from frozen, simply freeze after step 6, then when ready to cook, start at step 7, adding another 1 to 1½ hours cooking time.

✦ ✦ ✦

Baked Lokshyna (Butter-Fried Egg Noodle Casserole)

This dish is a traditional egg noodle casserole from the "old country" that has been adopted by many Canadian Prairie Ukrainians as a newer traditional Easter dish. Lokshyna means "noodles," and is very typical of how Ukrainians name their dishes—there are no fancy five-ingredient titles. Every Easter, my family picks and pokes at it when the dish is served during Easter dinner, taking only a few bites because we all know that the next day is when the real party starts. This dish firms up overnight, and the next day you can slice it and fry the slices in butter until the outsides are crisp, then eat it with leftover Easter ham and eggs for breakfast. This is my favorite thing to eat for breakfast once or twice a year. Note that lokshyna is not a casserole bursting with cheese flavor; it's more of a custard—which is what makes it so unique!

Makes 12 servings | Prep Time: 20 minutes | Total Time: 1 hour, 30 minutes

2 packages (12 oz/340 g each) broad egg noodles

¾ cup dry elbow macaroni

2 cups 2% milk

1 cup heavy cream

6 large eggs, beaten

2 tsp salt

3 cups packed shredded old cheddar cheese

◆ ◆ ◆

My Grandma Marion added elbow macaroni to the traditional recipe as she loved how they filled up the spaces between the egg noodles, making a firmer casserole. As always, her changes made it even better.

◆ ◆ ◆

1. Preheat the oven to 350°F. Grease and set aside a 2- × 9- × 13-inch pan.
2. Cook the egg noodles and elbow macaroni according to the package directions to al dente. Drain, then place in a very large mixing bowl.
3. Whisk together the milk, cream, eggs, and salt. Pour over the noodles. Add the cheese, then stir until the cheese and milk mixture are mixed throughout the noodles evenly.
4. Pour the noodle mixture into the prepared pan and spread out evenly. It will fill the entire pan perfectly. Cover with aluminum foil and bake for 50 minutes. Remove the foil and bake for another 20 minutes, or until a knife inserted comes out almost clean. You need to bake this to 165°F to cook the eggs properly.
5. Serve as a hot casserole immediately or refrigerate overnight. The next day, slice the lokshyna into ½-inch-thick slices. Melt 2 to 3 tablespoons of butter in a large frying pan and fry the pieces in the butter, turning to ensure both sides are crispy and brown. Serve hot with salt and pepper to taste.
6. This can be stored in the fridge for up to 3 days, but doesn't freeze well.

Perishke (Filled Buns)

These little buns can be filled with almost whatever your heart desires, but in my family, we love a cottage cheese and dill filling as well as a good basic cabbage one. You can also top them with the Ukrainian Onion, Cream, and Dill Sauce (page 25)—I'm pretty sure that perishke were the reason that sauce was invented. Each filling recipe makes enough for 24 perishke.

Makes 2 dozen perishke | Prep Time: 50 minutes | Total Time: 2 hours, 35 minutes, including rising

DOUGH

1 cup water, warmed to 115°F

½ cup plus 1 Tbsp white sugar

2 Tbsp traditional yeast

1 cup milk, scalded and cooled until just warm

3 eggs, beaten

6 Tbsp vegetable oil

6–6¼ cups all-purpose flour

1 tsp salt

COTTAGE CHEESE FILLING

2 (12 oz/375 g each) containers dry curd cottage cheese

1 cup finely chopped fresh dill

Salt and pepper

4 egg yolks

4 green onions, green part only, chopped (optional)

CABBAGE AND BACON FILLING

8 slices bacon, diced

6 cups diced green cabbage

1 large white onion, diced

Salt and pepper

1 batch Ukrainian Onion, Cream, and Dill Sauce (page 25) (optional)

1. Place the water, 1 tablespoon of the sugar, and the yeast in the bowl of a stand mixer fitted with a dough hook. Mix until just combined and then let stand until the mixture starts bubbling, around 5 minutes.

2. Mix in the remaining ½ cup of sugar, milk, eggs, and oil.

3. Whisk 2 cups of the flour with the salt, then add to the mixer bowl. Start the mixer on low to combine. Add the remaining flour 1 cup at a time, with the dough hook continuously mixing, until the dough is smooth, elastic, and slightly tacky to the touch. This may take up to 6¼ cups depending on the humidity of your kitchen. Knead for another 5 minutes, and then turn the dough out into a large, well-oiled mixing bowl. Cover with a clean, dry tea towel and place in a warm, draft-free area to rise until doubled in size, about 60 minutes.

4. During the rise, prepare your filling of choice.

5. To make the cottage cheese filling, combine the cottage cheese curds and dill in a medium-sized bowl. Add salt and pepper to taste—for the salt, start with 1 teaspoon; for the pepper, start with ¼ teaspoon. Once it is salty enough, add the egg yolks and mix in completely. Mash the curds with a fork to break them down slightly, then stir in the green onions. Refrigerate in an airtight container until you're ready to use. This can be made a day ahead of time.

see over

6. To make the cabbage and bacon filling, place the bacon, cabbage, and onion in a large skillet over medium-high heat and fry until the cabbage and onion are completely soft, about 20 minutes. Drain the grease. Add salt and pepper to taste. Set aside to cool or refrigerate if not using immediately. This can also be made a day ahead of time.

7. Once the dough has doubled in size, punch it down in the bowl. Flour your work surface lightly, then turn the dough out onto it. Divide the dough into 24 equal-sized pieces.

8. Flatten each piece into a disk about 2 inches wide. Take a tablespoon of your preferred filling (a cookie scoop works perfectly) and place it in the middle of the dough. Gather the dough around the filling, bunching together at the top. Pinch and seal the dough thoroughly at the top, then place the bun on a parchment-lined baking sheet, sealed side down. Repeat with all the pieces, placing 12 buns on each baking sheet. Cover lightly with a clean tea towel and let rise again in a warm, draft-free area until doubled in size, 45 to 50 minutes.

9. Preheat the oven to 350°F.

10. Bake the perishke for 15 to 20 minutes, until golden brown on top and bottom. Serve topped with the Ukrainian Onion, Cream, and Dill Sauce.

11. These can be eaten right away, stored in an airtight container in the fridge for 2 to 3 days, or frozen for up to 3 months. To freeze, let cool completely on the baking sheets, freeze on the baking sheets, and then transfer to freezer-safe bags. To cook from frozen, simply defrost and reheat in a 350°F oven until completely warmed through. Serve topped with the sauce.

Frog's Legs (Beet Leaf Buns)

Don't ask me why these are called "frog's legs" in my family because I simply don't have a clue other than that they are green. You may know them as perishke or beet leaf buns (the last one being the more accurate), which again shows you how varied these heritage recipes are in each family. Whatever you call them, these are made of a sweet dough wrapped in beet leaves, then smothered in a dill onion cream sauce. My family tends to tuck a juicy beet stem into the middle of the dough, which shows how innovative my relatives were in using every part of the plant possible in their cooking.

Makes 2 dozen buns | Prep Time: 2 hours | Total Time: 3 hours, 55 minutes

Dough

2 cups warm water (110°F)

½ cup white sugar

1½ Tbsp traditional yeast

¼ cup canola oil

1½ tsp salt

5–6 cups all-purpose flour

Beets

24 sections of juicy beet stem, each about 2 inches long

24–30 beet leaves, washed and dried (extra in case the leaves tear)

1 batch Ukrainian Onion, Cream, and Dill Sauce (page 25)

1. Place the water, sugar, and yeast in the bowl of a stand mixer fitted with a dough hook. Mix until just combined and then let stand until the mixture starts bubbling, around 5 minutes.

2. Mix in the oil and salt. With the mixer running on low speed, add the flour 1 cup at a time until the dough is smooth and slightly tacky to the touch. If needed, you may need to use all 6 cups of flour, depending on the humidity of your kitchen. Mix for another 5 minutes and then turn the dough out into a large, well-oiled mixing bowl. Drape with a clean, dry tea towel and place in a warm, draft-free area to rise for 50 to 60 minutes, or until it doubles in size.

3. Line 2 baking sheets with parchment paper.

4. Once the dough has doubled in size, punch it down in the bowl. Flour your work surface slightly, then turn the dough out onto it. Divide the dough into 24 equal-sized pieces.

5. Take each piece of dough and lay a 1-inch slice of beet stem in the middle, and then form into a log shape around the stem. The pieces should be around the same width as your beet leaves, as the dough will rise and expand outward later on. Gently massage and break the spines of the beet leaves so that they are bendable. Wrap them very loosely around the dough, placing them seam side down on the baking sheet and making sure that the leaf is secure. You want the leaf to be tucked firmly enough that it prevents the dough from rising up too much and instead directs it to rise out the sides.

see over

To make sure there is enough room for the dough to rise between the pieces, leave about 2 inches space around each piece. Cover each baking pan with a clean, dry tea towel and let the buns rise in a warm, draft-free spot until they fill up the space in the leaves, 50 to 60 minutes.

6. Preheat the oven to 350°F. Bake the buns for 20 to 25 minutes, until they are golden brown. Remove and cool on racks, if you're not planning to serve them hot.

7. To serve from either hot or cold, prepare 1 batch of the Ukrainian Onion, Cream, and Dill Sauce. Once ready, place one row of 8 buns on the bottom of a large greased roaster or casserole, large enough that you can fit 8 buns snugly together without being crowded. Pour a third of the hot sauce over top.

8. Repeat for another 2 layers, ending with a layer of sauce. If they are cold, heat in a 300°F oven until they are heated through to the middle. If they are hot, serve right after they are doused in the hot cream sauce.

9. These can be eaten right away, stored in an airtight container in the fridge for 2 to 3 days, or frozen for up to 3 months. To freeze, let cool completely on the baking sheets, freeze on the baking sheets, and then transfer to freezer-safe bags. To cook from frozen, simply defrost and reheat in the 350°F oven until heated through to the middle. Serve topped with sauce.

Borscht

Borscht is a polarizing soup: you either love it or hate it. I honestly think that the haters don't like it simply because it looks like the color of a car accident. What befuddles me is that so many people love beets, but won't touch borscht with a 10-foot pole. This dilly-delicious soup is so healthy and so popular with those who DO love it, you are sure to win a lot of hearts when you serve a big pot of it. While mine doesn't use meat, you do still need the beef broth for that traditional taste. If you do want to add more meat, you can; my Grandma Marion would use ground pork or beef in hers on rare occasions. You will also notice that there is no onion in this recipe, as my grandma never put it in! You can add in a cup of diced white onion if you are so inclined, but I find I prefer the earthy flavor of the beets as is.

Makes 8 servings | Prep Time: 20 minutes | Total Time: 1 hour to 1 hour, 10 minutes on stovetop or 6 hours, 20 minutes to 8 hours, 20 minutes in slow-cooker

8 cups strong beef broth

3 cups peeled, shredded beets

2 cups diced carrots

2 cups roughly chopped peeled red potatoes

1½ cups roughly chopped green beans

1 cup fresh baby peas

1 Tbsp fresh dill or 1 tsp dried dill

Sour cream, white vinegar, and dill, for garnish

1. Combine all the ingredients except the garnishes in a large stockpot. Bring to a boil and then turn down the heat to a simmer. Cover and continue to cook on medium heat until the vegetables are tender, 40 to 50 minutes. You can also cook on low in a slow cooker for 6 to 8 hours.
2. Serve in bowls with a splash of vinegar, a dollop of sour cream, and a sprinkle of dill.

✦ ✦ ✦

Traditionally borscht is made with a homemade beef broth base, but I prefer, for time and effort, to simply use powdered beef bouillon. If you want a lower-sodium version, you can use low-salt bouillon, but it does affect the final taste. I make my broth slightly stronger than the premade carton bouillon, as you need a good beefy base for the best taste. Whichever one you choose, make sure it has a good, beefy taste off the spoon, as this is the base for your soup.

✦ ✦ ✦

Nachynka (Cornbread Casserole)

This decadent cornmeal can act as a casserole or a stuffing. It is basically a Ukrainian polenta except it's creamier and richer thanks to the heavy dairy and eggs, which give it a glorious quiche texture. There are two versions: one with bacon and one without. It goes without saying which one I made and photographed here. Bacon for the win! Always. My Grandma Marion would make the meat-free version for Christmas as a stuffing. I adore cornmeal, so this is one of my very favorite dishes in this chapter! If you want, omit the bacon entirely and use butter instead of bacon drippings for the basic traditional dish.

Makes 6–8 servings | Prep Time: 15 minutes |
Total Time: 1 hour, 5 minutes to 1 hour, 15 minutes

6 slices good-quality bacon, chopped into small pieces (optional)

3 Tbsp butter (if not using bacon)

1 medium sweet white onion, grated (yields about ½ cup)

1 cup cornmeal

1 tsp salt

1 tsp white sugar

3½ cups milk

½ cup heavy cream

3 eggs, beaten

1. Preheat the oven to 350°F. Butter an 8-cup casserole dish.
2. If using the bacon, in a medium-sized stockpot over medium-high heat, fry the bacon until it is just slightly crispy but still soft. Drain, reserving 3 tablespoons of bacon drippings. Add the onion and sauté until soft.
3. Turn the heat to low and stir in the cornmeal, making sure that it is all covered in butter. Mix in the salt and sugar and remove the pot from the stove.
4. Pour the milk into a microwave-safe measuring cup. Microwave until the milk has scalded (it steams but does not boil), then add to the pot slowly, whisking continuously to prevent lumps. Return the pot to the stove and simmer on low heat for 4 to 5 minutes until the mixture thickens.
5. Remove from the heat and pour in the cream, whisking constantly until the mixture is smooth and creamy. Temper the eggs by whisking 3 tablespoons of the hot mixture into the beaten eggs, and then whisk the eggs back into the pot of cornmeal mixture.
6. Pour into the prepared casserole dish. Bake, uncovered, for 50 to 60 minutes, until a beautiful brown crust develops. Serve hot.
7. This will keep, covered, in the fridge for 2 to 3 days, but doesn't freeze that well.

Warm Polish Beet Salad and Chèvre

Aside from the chèvre (herbed goat cheese), which is my modern addition since beet salad traditionally has no cheese, this is pretty much as traditional a Ukrainian salad as you can get. It is one of my favorite healthy lunches to whip up during the week when I have beets available. The flavor reminds me of pickled beets, but served in a warm salad form with creamy cheese on top.

Makes 2–4 servings | Prep Time: 10 | Total Time: 25 to 35 minutes

2 Tbsp extra-virgin olive oil

1 yellow onion, finely chopped

4 cups peeled, shredded beets

¼ cup water

3 Tbsp white vinegar

2 Tbsp honey

Salt

Minced fresh dill

1½-inch-wide round of herbed goat cheese

1. Heat the oil in a medium skillet over medium heat.
2. Add the chopped onions and sauté until tender.
3. Add the beets, water, and vinegar. Cover with a lid and steam the beets until tender-crisp, 5 to 7 minutes.
4. Add the honey, then salt to taste. Cook, uncovered, for another 10 to 15 minutes until the beets are soft.
5. Slice the goat cheese into 5 to 6 rounds, then place on top of the beets. Cover and remove from the heat. Let the cheese warm up and melt slightly, then garnish with dill. Serve onto plates from the skillet.

✦ ✦ ✦

If you are serving this cold, cook the beets and keep them in the fridge until the next day. To prevent the cheese from getting soggy, slice the goat cheese and mix it into the cold beets right before serving.

✦ ✦ ✦

Medivnyk (Ukrainian Honey Cake)

If there is one ingredient other than saskatoon berries that Canadian settlers used in their baking on a regular basis, it's honey. Honey was more available in tough times than white sugar was, not to mention cheaper if you kept your own bees or had a neighbor who did and was willing to trade. Honey features prominently in many Prairie desserts, from bars to cakes to cookies. This honey cake is one that is sure to impress. The mild honey and coffee flavor is unique, and the honey cream cheese glaze (my addition) makes it perfect. Traditionally, you need buckwheat honey to get that rich flavor in the cake, but feel free to taste-test with your favorite type. You can choose to use buckwheat honey in the glaze as well, but I prefer a sweeter, lighter honey like clover.

Makes 12–16 slices | Prep Time: 15 minutes | Total Time: 2 hours

Honey Cake

½ cup butter, room temperature

1 cup packed brown sugar

4 eggs

1 cup honey

3 cups all-purpose flour

3 Tbsp cornstarch

2 tsp baking powder

1 tsp baking soda

1 tsp ground cinnamon

½ tsp salt

¼ tsp ground cloves

½ cup sour cream

½ cup strong black coffee, cooled

Honey Cream Cheese Glaze

1 package (8 oz/226 g) cream cheese, softened

¼ cup honey

¼ cup icing sugar

1–3 Tbsp heavy cream

1. Preheat the oven to 325°F. Grease a 10-inch Bundt pan with butter or cooking spray.
2. Place the butter in the bowl of a stand mixer fitted with the paddle attachment. Beat the butter to soften it, and then add the brown sugar. Beat them together until light and creamy. Beat in the eggs 1 at a time, until fully incorporated. Add the honey and mix well.
3. In a medium bowl, whisk together the flour, cornstarch, baking powder, baking soda, cinnamon, salt, and cloves until combined.
4. Combine the sour cream and coffee in a liquid measuring cup.
5. Beat one-third of the dry ingredients into the butter mixture, followed by one-third of the liquid mixture. Repeat twice, ending with the last of the liquid mixture.
6. Pour the batter into the prepared Bundt pan. Tap the pan gently on the counter to release any air bubbles, and then place it in the oven.
7. Bake for 55 to 65 minutes, until a cake tester comes out clean. As with all Bundt cakes, check in the middle of the cake and also by the inner tube for doneness.
8. Let cool in the pan for 10 minutes and then invert onto a wire rack to cool completely. Wrap in plastic wrap to keep moist.

see over

9. To make the glaze, combine the cream cheese, honey, and icing sugar in a medium-sized bowl. Using a hand mixer or stand mixer, beat the mixture until creamy and smooth. Add the cream, 1 tablespoon at a time, until the glaze reaches your desired consistency. Adjust the sweetness by adding more icing sugar if needed and balancing the consistency with a bit more cream.

10. Pour the glaze over the cake and let set for a few minutes. Slice and serve.

11. This cake will last for 2 to 3 days in the fridge, or wrap the unfrosted cake tightly in plastic wrap, then in aluminum foil, and freeze for up to 3 months.

CARBS, CARBS, DELICIOUS CARBS

I'd venture a guess that to most people there is nothing as heavenly as the smell of fresh buns or bread baking first thing in the morning. To me that aroma always seems to herald the beginning of the weekend or a holiday. It brings forth warm fuzzy feelings of lazy mornings spent in pajamas, drinking too much coffee (spiked with Irish cream on holidays, of course), and baking with the kids.

Also, I like carbs. A LOT.

We do try to eat easy, high-protein, vegetable-based meals during the week. However, on the weekend all bets are off. It's when we indulge in freshly baked breads, buns, scones, and some butter. It's the perfect time to make my Grandma Marion's aptly named Grandma Marion's Weekend Buns, on page 58, which can then be enjoyed during the week as they freeze (and thaw) exceptionally well. The kids like to pack them in their school lunches or use them to make sandwiches or breakfast egg buns for a quick morning meal.

My go-to, however, is always to bake up a batch of The Best Scones. Ever. (page 53). I have been baking this recipe all my life—I couldn't even tell you which grandma it came from, or which one gave it to my mom. It's always just been called the "sour cream scones" recipe in my family. As most of our family recipes tend to be, it was just a list of ingredients and a few instructions. I've tweaked the recipe to include modern knowledge, such as using cold butter, and I have perfected a foolproof method for forming and cutting scones—no scouring the top of dough disks before they bake, or rolling out and cutting squares. The scones are always the correct size, so no small scones that dry out or large ones that don't bake properly, folks.

Once you learn this method, you will never go back.

◆ ◆ ◆

How to Make Perfect Scones

➤ *Once the dough has been combined, form into a log that is evenly sized all the way around.*

➤ *For a 12-scone yield, cut the dough log into 2 equal pieces. For an 18-scone yield, cut the log into 3 equal pieces. For recipes that aren't mine and yield other numbers, round to the nearest of the numbers I give here; you will just get slightly larger or smaller scones.*

➤ *Flatten each piece of dough into a disk that is 1 inch high and, depending on the recipe, anywhere from 4 to 8 inches wide. What you are looking for is the height of 1 inch, with the resulting circle width being a fluid measurement. Make sure each disk is a relatively even 1-inch thickness from the outside edge to the middle; do not make thin edges. This will ensure that the scones are the same thickness for baking and keeps your scones flaky by preventing overworking of the dough.*

➤ *Cut each disk into 6 evenly sized triangles, and follow your recipe's baking instructions.*

◆ ◆ ◆

Faux Sourdough Bread (page 62)

The Best Scones. Ever.

My family has used this scone recipe for as long as I can remember, even though it's a bit of an odd one. It makes 18 scones (instead of the standard 12) and has sour cream paired with baking soda to give it some extra "lift." This recipe yields a crisp, snappy buttery scone that has absolutely no cakiness to it whatsoever, something that makes or breaks a scone for me! And these are without a doubt Mr. Kitchen Magpie's very favorite carb treat. So much so that's he's mastered baking them for himself so he always has a regular supply.

Makes 18 scones | Prep Time: 15 minutes | Total Time: 35 minutes

1 cup sour cream

1 tsp baking soda

4 cups all-purpose flour

1 cup white sugar

2 tsp baking powder

1 tsp salt

1 cup cold butter, cut into cubes or grated with a box grater

1 egg, beaten

Milk, as needed

1 cup currants, Thompson raisins, or dried blueberries

1. Preheat the oven to 350°F. Line 2 baking sheets with parchment paper.
2. Combine the sour cream and baking soda in a small bowl. Set aside.
3. Whisk together the flour, sugar, baking powder, and salt in a large mixing bowl.
4. Cut in the butter using a pastry blender or 2 knives in a criss-cross fashion, until the butter is broken into pea-sized morsels in the flour.
5. Mix the egg into the sour cream. Add the sour cream mixture to the dry mixture, working it in. The dough can be a bit dry, but if you use your hands to combine it, it will be perfect. If necessary, add a tiny amount of milk, 1 teaspoon at a time, until it's combined. The secret to a good scone is a drier dough, not a gluey one.
6. Once the mixture is almost completely combined, add your fruit of choice, then finish mixing, until the fruit is mixed evenly throughout.
7. Using a lightly floured work surface, follow the instructions on page 50 to cut out 18 triangular scones.
8. Bake 1 inch apart on the parchment-lined baking sheets for 15 to 20 minutes, until the scones are browned nicely on the bottom and slightly brown on top. Watch them carefully!
9. Serve and enjoy.
10. These can be stored at room temperature in an airtight container for 2 to 3 days, or frozen in a freezer-safe container or bag for up to 3 months.

Cranberry Orange Scones

Have a craving for a scone but don't have sour cream in the fridge (nor anyone who wants to run to the store on a Sunday morning to get them)? Have no fear. This scone recipe uses cream instead, or even milk in a pinch, which almost all of us usually have on hand. Not only that, but this is an excellent base recipe, meaning you can substitute any dried fruit for the cranberries. You can also play around with the liquid base and use all cream if you have no juice, or use a large lemon and substitute lemon juice and zest in place of the orange to create another amazing taste combination.

Makes 1 dozen scones | Prep Time: 15 minutes | Total Time: 30 minutes

Scones

3½ cups all-purpose flour

¾ cup white sugar

2½ Tbsp baking powder

1 tsp salt

Zest of 1 medium orange

⅔ cup cold butter

2 eggs, beaten

½ cup cream (heavy or light)

½ cup orange juice

1 cup sweetened dried cranberries

Tangy Orange Glaze

1 cup icing sugar

1 Tbsp melted salted butter, cooled until just warm

1–2 Tbsp orange juice

1–2 Tbsp orange zest or other citrus zest

1. Preheat the oven to 400°F.
2. To make the scones, in a large mixing bowl, whisk together the flour, sugar, baking powder, and salt. Mix in the orange zest.
3. Using a box grater, shred in the cold butter, then, using a pastry blender or 2 knives in a criss-cross fashion, mix in well, making sure there are no pieces larger than a pea.
4. Whisk the eggs, cream, and orange juice together. Pour the mixture into the dry ingredients and mix gently with a wooden spoon, bringing the dough together until almost completely combined. Then add the cranberries and finish mixing.
5. Using a lightly floured work surface, follow the instructions on page 50 to cut out 12 triangular scones.
6. Place all 12 scones on a parchment-lined baking sheet, leaving a 1-inch space between them.
7. Bake for 18 to 20 minutes, until deep brown on top.
8. Transfer to a wire rack to cool completely.
9. To make the glaze, whisk the glaze ingredients together, and then drizzle over the completely cooled scones. Let the glaze set slightly. Serve with jam and butter.
10. These can be stored at room temperature in an airtight container for 2 to 3 days, or frozen in a freezer-safe container or bag for up to 3 months.

Chocolate Zucchini Scones

Here's a perfect way to use up your garden zucchini. These aren't super-sweet scones, and they're likely to appeal to cocoa lovers. The dough is quite dry when you are working it, but bakes up crispy on the outside and cakey on the inside, so here's a recipe for the cakey scone lovers out there!

Makes 18 scones | Prep Time: 15 minutes | Total Time: 35 minutes

4 cups all-purpose flour

1 cup white sugar

½ cup Dutch process cocoa powder

2 tsp baking powder

1 tsp baking soda

1 tsp salt

1 cup cold butter

1 cup peeled, shredded zucchini

1 egg, beaten well

½ cup sour cream

¼ cup finishing or sanding sugar to top

1. Preheat the oven to 375°F. Line a baking sheet with parchment paper.
2. Place the flour, sugar, cocoa powder, baking powder, baking soda, and salt in the bowl of a stand mixer. Whisk together by hand, then fit the paddle attachment to the mixer.
3. Using a box grater, grate the butter into the dry mixture, then mix on low speed until incorporated.
4. Add the zucchini and mix until incorporated.
5. Combine the egg and sour cream, then add to the bowl. Mix on low speed until the dough comes together. It will be a very dry dough.
6. Remove from the bowl and knead a few times. Form into a log, then cut into 3 equal pieces. Flatten each piece into a circle about 5 inches wide and 1 inch thick. Cut into 6 triangles.
7. Place the scones 1 inch apart on the prepared baking sheet and sprinkle with the finishing sugar. Bake for 20 to 22 minutes, until they are browned and crispy when tapped on the outside. Let cool to the touch on the baking sheet and then transfer to wire racks to cool completely.
8. These can be stored at room temperature in an airtight container for 2 to 3 days, or frozen in a freezer-safe container or bag for up to 3 months.

Grandma Marion's Weekend Buns

I'm pretty sure the point of this cookbook was to share the recipe for my Grandma Marion's Weekend Buns. These buns are the softest, most decadent buns you'll ever bake up. My grandma's trick for added flavor was using rendered chicken fat—which is our closely guarded family secret ingredient! The combination of that with the butter and lard is what makes these buns so special.

Makes 4 dozen buns | Prep Time: 40 minutes | Total Time: 2 hours, 40 minutes

Buns

4 cups whole milk, scalded and cooled to 105°F–110°F

1½ Tbsp traditional yeast

1 cup white sugar

1 cup butter, melted and cooled until just warm

¼ cup non-hydrogenated lard, melted and cooled until just warm

2 Tbsp rendered chicken fat, cooled

1 egg yolk, beaten

1¾ Tbsp salt

11–12 cups all-purpose flour

Sugar Butter Glaze

1 cup salted butter, softened

¼ cup white sugar

◆ ◆ ◆

To make this dough ahead, or save some for later, let the dough rise once, then shape it into balls and freeze solid on sheets. Transfer to a plastic bag and freeze for up to 4 weeks. To use, defrost it and continue the recipe starting at step 7.

◆ ◆ ◆

1. Grease four 9- × 13-inch baking pans or baking sheets.
2. Attach the dough hook to your stand mixer and place the bowl on the stand. Oil the dough hook to prevent the dough from sticking. Combine the milk, yeast, and sugar in the stand mixer bowl and let stand until mixture bubbles, about 5 minutes.
3. Mix in the butter, lard, chicken fat, and egg on low speed.
4. With the mixer running on medium speed, add the salt, then slowly add 11 cups of the flour, 1 cup at a time. Add extra flour, 2 tablespoons at a time, until the dough is slightly tacky to the touch. Combine, and then let the dough hook knead the dough for an extra 4 to 5 minutes.
5. Turn out dough onto a floured work surface, knead for 1 to 2 minutes, then shape into a large ball. Place in a large oiled bowl and cover with a clean, dry tea towel. Let rise in a warm, draft-free place for 1 hour or until doubled in size.
6. Punch down the dough. Turn the dough out on a well-floured work surface. Divide into 4 equal parts. Divide each of those pieces into 12 balls and roll until smooth in shape.
7. Place 12 dough balls into each prepared baking pan. Cover the pans with clean, dry tea towels and let rise again in a warm place for 1 hour or until doubled in size.
8. Preheat the oven to 400°F.
9. Bake the rolls, 2 pans at a time on the same oven shelf, for 14 to 15 minutes, until they are very golden brown and the tops sound hollow when tapped.
10. To make the glaze, mix together the butter and sugar until incorporated.
11. Remove the buns from the oven and brush the tops with the glaze, allowing it to be absorbed.

12. Cool in the pans. These can be stored at room temperature in an airtight container for 2 to 3 days, or frozen in a freezer-safe container or bag for up to 3 months.

You can get fatty chicken scraps from any local butcher or even your local grocery store. To render chicken fat, cook 1 pound of fatty chicken scraps over very low heat in a skillet until the chicken skin is browned and crisp and the fat is clear and liquid. Drain the fat through a fine-mesh strainer into a glass jar and cool until solid. You can keep it, sealed, in your fridge for a month or your freezer for up to a year. Depending on the chicken, you can get as much as 1 cup of fat. You can salt the remaining crispy chicken skin and eat it as a snack or a topping for salads.

Hawaiian Sweet Buns

These are a copycat version of one of my favorite dinner buns that you can usually only buy in the United States. My entire family loves them, and we get our fix when we are there. I combined my Grandma Marion's secret of using scalded milk and egg yolks for the richest bread possible with pineapple juice (I figured it has to be the secret sweet ingredient in Hawaiian buns, right?) and voilà! Hawaiian buns to tide us over until we get to the States again!

Makes 2 dozen buns | Prep Time: 40 minutes | Total Time: 2 hours, 50 minutes, including rising

1 cup pineapple juice

1 cup whole milk

¾ cup white sugar

½ cup butter

4½ tsp traditional yeast

2 eggs

2 egg yolks

½ tsp vanilla extract

6 cups all-purpose flour

1 tsp salt

◆ ◆ ◆

The secret to using pineapple juice in a bread recipe is that you have to heat it up to break down the enzymes, or they can interfere with the yeast-rising process.

◆ ◆ ◆

1. Microwave the pineapple juice in a microwave-safe measuring cup for 2 minutes, and then let cool until lukewarm.
2. Combine the milk, sugar, and butter in a large glass measuring cup. Microwave in 60-second increments until the butter melts and the milk is steamy but not boiling. Pour this warm liquid into the bowl of a stand mixer and let cool to 115°F. Stir in the yeast by hand and wait for it to start bubbling, about 5 minutes.
3. Beat the eggs and the egg yolks together in a small bowl, then stir in the cooled pineapple juice and the vanilla. Stir by hand into the yeast mixture.
4. Attach the dough hook to your stand mixer and place the bowl on the stand. Oil the dough hook to prevent the dough from sticking. Mix 2 cups of the flour with the salt, add to the yeast mixture in the bowl, and start the mixer on the slowest speed. Mix, slowly adding more flour ½ cup at a time until the dough reaches a slightly tacky consistency. Add more flour 2 tablespoons at a time if needed until the desired tackiness has been reached.
5. Form the dough into a ball and place it in a large oiled bowl. Drape a clean, dry tea towel overtop and let rise in a warm, draft-free area until the dough has doubled in size, around 60 minutes.
6. Grease two 9- × 13-inch baking pans.
7. Punch down the dough and split into 2 evenly sized pieces. Make 12 small balls from each piece, making sure the tops are smooth. Place 12 dough balls into each pan, spacing 3 apart in a row across and 4 in a row for the length.

8. Cover loosely with plastic wrap and place in the same warm area again. Let rise until doubled in size, 70 to 80 minutes.

9. Preheat the oven to 350°F.

10. Bake the buns for 20 to 25 minutes or until they are brown on top and sound hollow-ish when tapped on top. Remove from the pans and cool on wire racks.

11. Store in airtight containers at room temperature for up to 3 days or freeze in freezer-safe containers or bags for up to 2 months.

Faux Sourdough Bread

I really want to be able to keep a sourdough starter. I do. I have tried numerous times over the years, and I've ruined them all. I even had one of my favorite local restaurants give me a piece from their "mother"—that's what they called their starter—that makes the best sourdough ever.

I killed mother. Dead. I haven't looked the chef in the eye and told him, but he'll read this.

Until I learn how to perfect a starter, this faux sourdough recipe is for everyone like me. It's a coarse-crumbed yet surprisingly airy bread, with a sour tang and crispy crust. It's as close as I can get to the real thing until I pay someone to make me sourdough daily, which I'm working on—any takers?

Makes 1 loaf of bread | Prep Time: 2 hours, 30 minutes |
Total Time: 3 hours, including rising

¾ cup water, heated to 110°F –115°F

1 Tbsp white traditional yeast

1 Tbsp white sugar

1½ cups full-fat sour cream

1 Tbsp white vinegar

2 Tbsp vegetable oil

2 tsp salt

4–4¼ cups all-purpose flour

1. Place water in the bowl of a stand mixer. Add the yeast and sugar and stir to combine. Let stand until the yeast starts to bubble, around 5 minutes.

2. In a large, microwave-safe measuring cup, combine the sour cream and vinegar. Heat slightly in the microwave until warm, about 30 seconds, then stir in the oil. Add to the yeast mixture and gently mix in by hand.

3. Stir the salt into 2 cups of the flour, then using a hook attachment and using the lowest setting of the mixer slowly mix in the flour. Add another 2 cups of flour, 1 at a time, while the mixer is running, until the dough comes together in a sticky dough. Add just enough flour until it sticks to your hands and the bowl slightly more than usual. You may not need all 4 cups as this is a wet dough. Let the mixer knead the dough for 5 minutes, then form the dough into a ball and place it in a large oiled bowl. Drape a clean, dry tea towel overtop and let rise in a warm, draft-free area until the dough has doubled in size, 60 to 80 minutes.

4. Line a 12-inch-diameter Dutch oven with parchment paper.

5. Turn the dough out onto a lightly floured work surface. The dough will start falling as soon as you take it out of the bowl. Fold the dough over into the middle 4 times. Looking at the dough as a compass, take the north edge, pull it out slightly, then bring it back over itself, creating a double layer and slight air pocket and pulling the edge back to the middle. Rotating the dough, repeat with the remaining 3 points, gathering all of the edges into the middle again. You are essentially trying to make a few air pockets by stretching the dough out and folding it over itself again. Once done, turn the dough over so that the smooth side is facing up, and tuck the rough edges under, forming the dough into an 11-inch dome.

6. Place the dough in the middle of the parchment paper in the Dutch oven.

7. Set the oven rack in the middle and set the Dutch oven on the rack with the lid on.

8. Let the dough double in size, around 60 minutes, and then start the oven at 450°F, leaving the Dutch oven inside. Once the oven reaches 450°F, bake for 25 minutes, then remove the lid. Continue to bake for another 25 to 30 minutes, until the top is golden brown and the bread sounds hollow when you tap it.

9. Remove from the oven and cool the bread on a wire rack. Slice and enjoy.

10. This bread can be kept in an airtight container or sealed bag for 3 to 4 days at room temperature or frozen for up to 3 months.

Bakery-Style Blueberry Muffins

There are a few bakers' tricks to make these muffins taste like they are from a bakery. First, use almond extract to enhance the blueberry flavor. Second, a little cornstarch makes a cupcake-like texture. Third, the finishing sugar adds a sweet crunch on top. Fresh blueberries will then give you that coveted juicy, fruity "pop" but frozen blueberries will do in a pinch.

Makes 1 dozen muffins | Prep Time: 15 minutes | Total Time: 35 to 40 minutes

2 cups all-purpose flour

2 Tbsp cornstarch

2 tsp baking powder

½ tsp salt

¼ cup butter, softened

½ cup vegetable oil

1 cup white sugar

2 large eggs

1½ tsp vanilla extract

½ tsp almond extract

½ cup whole milk

2 cups fresh blueberries

½ cup white finishing sugar, for garnish

♦ ♦ ♦

Muffin Making Tip

A #8 food disher or ice cream scoop makes bakery-style, evenly sized dome-topped muffins every time!

♦ ♦ ♦

1. Preheat the oven to 375°F.
2. Fill a 12-cup muffin tin with muffin liners or spray the muffin cups with nonstick cooking spray.
3. In a medium bowl, whisk together the flour, cornstarch, baking powder, and salt.
4. Using a stand mixer fitted with the paddle attachment, or a large bowl and a handheld mixer, beat the butter until softened. Add the oil and sugar and beat for 2 minutes, until creamy.
5. Add the eggs 1 at a time, scraping down the sides of the bowl and beating well after each addition, then beat in the vanilla and almond extracts.
6. With the mixer running on low speed, gradually add the flour mixture and milk, alternating between the two, in 3 additions ending with the milk.
7. Fold in the blueberries until evenly mixed throughout.
8. Divide the batter evenly between the muffin cups using a #8 food disher or ice cream scoop.
9. Sprinkle desired amount of finishing sugar on top of the muffins.
10. Bake for 20 to 25 minutes, until the tops are beautifully browned and spring back when touched. Insert a cake tester or a toothpick into the middle of the muffins ensuring no crumbs are attached when removed.
11. Remove from the oven and cool on a wire rack.
12. Store in an airtight container for 3 to 4 days or freeze in a sealed container for up to a month. I find muffins can take on odors in a freezer, so they shouldn't be frozen for too long.

Pumpkin Morning Glory Muffins

My pumpkin version of morning glory muffins was whipped up as a treat for the ward staff at a local hospital who were taking care of a relative at the time. I wanted to create a treat that was sweet but relatively healthy and full of energy-boosting goodness, as I know that they tend to get a lot of sugar-laden treats. These muffins were gone in mere minutes, with rave reviews from the staff. These have become my go-to thank-you gift/treat for when I don't want to give something sugary. This recipe yields 2 dozen as they are fiddly to make and my theory is if you are messing up the kitchen anyway, bake a large batch and freeze some for later.

Makes 2 dozen muffins | Prep Time: 30 minutes, including shredding the fruits and vegetables | Total Time: 50 minutes

2¼ cups whole-wheat flour

1 cup all-purpose flour

1 cup packed brown sugar

¼ cup white sugar

1½ Tbsp baking powder

1 Tbsp baking soda

1 Tbsp pumpkin spice

1 tsp ground cinnamon

1 tsp salt

1 cup canned pumpkin puree (not pie filling)

½ cup melted butter

¼ cup vegetable oil

2 eggs, beaten

1½ Tbsp vanilla extract

2 cups shredded carrots

1 cup shredded, peeled apple (sweet is the best)

1 cup raisins, dark or golden

½ cup shredded sweetened coconut

½ cup chopped walnuts

Raw pepitas (shelled pumpkin seeds), for garnish

1. Preheat the oven to 375°F.
2. Line the cups of two 12-cup muffin tins with paper liners.
3. In a large mixing bowl, whisk together both flours, both sugars, the baking powder, baking soda, pumpkin spice, cinnamon, and salt. Set aside.
4. In a medium bowl, mix the pumpkin puree, butter, oil, eggs, and vanilla extract together until well combined. Stir in the carrots and apple. Mix this into the dry ingredients until just combined, then stir in the raisins, coconut, and walnuts until just mixed in.
5. Divide the batter evenly between the muffin cups using a #8 food disher or ice cream scoop.
6. Top each muffin with 6 to 8 pepitas. Bake for 18 to 20 minutes, or until the tops are fully cooked and a cake tester or toothpick inserted in the center of a muffin comes out clean.
7. Remove from the muffin pans and cool on wire racks.
8. Store in a sealed container for 3 to 4 days or freeze in a sealed container for up to a month. I find muffins can take on odors in a freezer, so they shouldn't be frozen for too long.

Orange and Brown Sugar Cinnamon Buns

Old-fashioned cinnamon buns always have an orange-flavored frosting on top in my oldest cookbooks—most likely because oranges were a common and affordable fruit readily available to most Prairie households during the early and mid-1900s. Even still, we don't have access to every fruit year-round. Heck, have you ever tried finding raspberries in the stores in December? Impossible. I wanted to recreate that vintage taste with a new recipe combining the caramel notes of brown sugar with the sweet tang of orange juice. These cinnamon buns bake up with their own ready-made orange-flavored topping, so you don't have to frost them afterward. This recipe yields 12 buns and doubles perfectly if you are making it for a larger crowd!

Makes 1 dozen buns | Prep Time: 2 hours, 20 minutes |
Total Time: 2 hours, 45 minutes, including rising

DOUGH

¼ cup warm water (110°F)

2¼ tsp traditional yeast

¼ cup scalded milk, cooled until lukewarm

¼ cup white sugar

½ tsp salt

1 large egg, beaten

¼ cup melted butter

2¼–2½ cups all-purpose flour

FILLING

2 Tbsp softened butter

½ cup packed brown sugar

2 tsp ground cinnamon

ORANGE BROWN SUGAR SAUCE

1 cup packed brown sugar

½ cup sweetened pulp-free orange juice

2–3 Tbsp grated orange zest (plus extra for topping if desired)

1. Attach the dough hook to your stand mixer and place the bowl on the stand. Oil the dough hook to prevent the dough from sticking. Combine the warm water and yeast in the stand mixer bowl and let stand until the mixture bubbles, about 5 minutes.

2. Add the milk, white sugar, salt, egg, and melted butter and stir by hand.

3. Add 2 cups of the flour, then, using the lowest mixer speed, mix until the flour is incorporated.

4. Add enough of the remaining ½ cup of flour, 1 tablespoon at a time, to bring the dough together, until it's smooth and elastic and only slightly tacky to the touch.

5. Place in an oiled bowl, drape a clean, dry tea towel over top, and let rise in a warm, draft-free place until doubled in size, about 60 minutes.

6. Punch down the dough and turn it out onto a floured work surface. Roll it out into a 10- × 12-inch rectangle.

7. For the filling, spread the butter on top of the rectangle using the back of a spoon. Mix together the brown sugar and cinnamon and sprinkle it over the butter.

see over

8. Holding the long side of the dough (meaning that you are going to end up with a roll that is 12 inches long, not 10), roll it up tightly into a log. Pinch the seam and roll the log so that the seam is at the bottom.

9. Slice into twelve 1-inch-wide rolls.

10. Whisk together the ingredients for the Orange Brown Sugar Sauce. Pour into the bottom of a 9- × 13-inch pan. (This recipe is too big for a round pan.)

11. Place the 12 cinnamon buns (cut side down for the end pieces) on top of the sauce.

12. Cover loosely with plastic wrap and let rise until the buns fill the pan entirely, 50 to 60 minutes.

13. Preheat the oven to 375°F.

14. Bake the cinnamon buns for 25 to 30 minutes, until browned on top and baked through.

15. Remove, flipping the buns over onto a plate or tray. Top with additional orange zest if desired and serve warm.

16. These can be stored at room temperature in an airtight container for 2 to 3 days, or frozen in a freezer-safe container for up to 3 months. Let's be honest: if you can ignore cinnamon buns in the freezer for 3 months, you are a stronger person than me.

Banana Gingerbread Loaf

If you are a loyal reader of my website, the Kitchen Magpie, you will know that I am always on a quest to invent delicious ways to use up my freezer bananas. Freezer bananas are those bananas that we throw into our freezers with the good intention of baking with them some day. Well, you know the saying about which road is paved with good intentions? It's no different in my house. I have good banana-baking intentions, which led me to coming up with all sorts of ways to use them up. What better to enhance the banana flavor than molasses and spices? This is a deep, dark, and delicious loaf that has become my new go-to freezer banana recipe. The best part? It uses up to 7 freezer bananas and makes 2 loaves.

Makes 2 loaves | Prep Time: 15 minutes |
Total Time: 1 hour, 5 minutes to 1 hour, 15 minutes

¾ cup butter, softened

1 cup packed brown sugar (can be replaced with white sugar for a sweeter loaf)

2 eggs

3 cups mashed bananas (6–7 medium bananas)

1 cup molasses (cooking molasses for a deep dark flavor; fancy molasses for a lighter flavor)

3 cups all-purpose flour

1 tsp baking powder

1 tsp baking soda

2½ tsp ground ginger

2 tsp ground cinnamon

1 tsp ground cloves

½ tsp ground nutmeg

1. Preheat the oven to 350°F. Grease and flour two 9¼- × 5¼-inch loaf pans.
2. Using a stand mixer fitted with the paddle attachment, or a large bowl and handheld mixer, beat the butter with the sugar until light and fluffy.
3. Beat in the eggs at medium speed until combined, then add the banana and molasses and continue mixing until completely combined.
4. In a medium-sized bowl, whisk the flour, baking powder, and baking soda with the ginger, cinnamon, cloves, and nutmeg.
5. Add the dry ingredients to the wet mixture and beat on low speed until just completely mixed in.
6. Divide the batter evenly between the 2 loaf pans and bake for 50 to 60 minutes, or until a cake tester inserted comes out clean.
7. Remove and cool in the pans for 10 to 15 minutes, then transfer from the pans onto wire racks and cool completely.
8. These loaves will last for 2 to 3 days in your refrigerator, or wrap each tightly in plastic wrap, then in aluminum foil, and freeze for up to 3 months.

Dill Monkey Bread

Homemade monkey bread (that means the dough doesn't come out of a can) is one of my favorite things to bake on the weekend. We usually make a sweet monkey bread on Sunday mornings, but when trying to think of a new savory version, my Ukrainian mind went straight to dill. Just dill. No cheese, no garlic, no other spices (although you can play around with the herbs in this recipe if you want to). This monkey bread is amazing by itself, but when paired with the 2-for-1 Dill Pickle Dip (see page 96), it's a dill lover's paradise.

Makes 8 servings | Prep Time: 25 minutes | Total Time: 2 hours, 25 minutes, including rising

DOUGH

1 cup milk, warmed to 115°F

⅓ cup water, warmed to 115°F

2 Tbsp melted butter

3 Tbsp white sugar

2¼ tsp rapid-rise yeast

¼ cup chopped fresh dill or
    2 Tbsp freeze-dried dill

3¼ cups all-purpose flour, plus
    2 Tbsp if needed

2 tsp salt

TOPPING

½ cup melted butter

2 Tbsp chopped fresh or 1 Tbsp
    freeze-dried dill

Melted butter and sea salt,
    if desired

1. To make the dough, in a large liquid measuring cup, mix together the milk, water, melted butter, sugar, and yeast. Let sit until the yeast foams, then mix in the chopped dill.

2. In the bowl of a stand mixer, whisk together the flour and salt by hand. Attach the dough hook.

3. With the mixer running on its lowest speed, slowly add the milk mixture. After the dough has come together, increase the speed to medium and let your dough hook do the work until the dough is shiny and smooth, 6 to 7 minutes. The dough should be slightly sticky, but if it is too wet to come together into a ball, add an additional 2 tablespoons of flour. The dough should just barely stick to your hands, nothing more. Turn the dough onto a lightly floured counter and knead for about 30 seconds to form a smooth, round ball.

4. Take the ball of dough and place in an oiled bowl. Drape a clean, dry towel over top and let rise in a warm, draft-free place until doubled in size, 45 to 50 minutes.

5. Grease a standard Bundt pan and set aside.

6. Transfer the dough to a lightly floured work surface. Tear the dough into about 40 evenly sized pieces and roll each one into a ball.

◆ ◆ ◆

While I do make this with only dill, you can add some garlic, oregano, Italian seasoning, or whatever spice is your favorite.

◆ ◆ ◆

7. For the topping, place the melted butter in a bowl, then mix in the dill.
8. Dip each dough ball in the butter and dill mixture, roll it around to coat evenly, then place it in the Bundt pan, staggering the layers like bricks in a wall. Once finished, drape a clean, dry towel over top and let rise again in a warm, draft-free place until the bread reaches the top of the Bundt pan, around 40 minutes.
9. Preheat the oven to 350°F.
10. Bake for 30 to 35 minutes, until the bread is nicely browned on top and the dough has pulled away from the sides of the pan.
11. Remove, let cool for 5 minutes, and then invert onto a plate. If desired, brush the bread with melted butter and sprinkle sea salt before serving.
12. This can be stored at room temperature in an airtight container or wrapped in plastic wrap for 2 to 3 days, or frozen in a freezer-safe container or bag for up to 3 months.

Pumpkin Pull-Apart Biscuits

Pumpkin is such a delightfully versatile ingredient. I always have some on hand in my pantry ready for when I need a pumpkin fix. I whipped up these skillet biscuits merely to use up some leftover pumpkin—the rest had made it into the muffins on page 66—and it ended up being a cookbook-worthy recipe. Eat these as you would cornbread, and pair them with chilis or sweeter soups like butternut squash.

Makes 12 biscuits | Prep Time: 10 minutes | Total Time: 30 minutes

1¾ cups all-purpose flour

¾ cup packed brown sugar

2½ tsp baking powder

¼ tsp baking soda

½ tsp salt

½ tsp ground cinnamon

¼ tsp ground nutmeg

½ cup cold or frozen butter

¾ cup canned pumpkin (not pie filling)

⅓ cup milk

1 tsp vanilla extract (omit if pairing with savory dishes)

1. Preheat the oven to 400°F.
2. In a large bowl, place the flour, sugar, baking powder, baking soda, salt, cinnamon, and nutmeg. Whisk until combined.
3. Using a box grater, shred in the cold butter. Then, using a pastry blender or 2 knives in a criss-cross fashion, mix in well, making sure there are no pieces larger than a pea.
4. Mix the pumpkin, milk, and vanilla in a liquid measuring cup, then, using a wooden spoon, stir into the dry ingredients until just moistened. Use your hands to bring the dough together in a ball, trying not to overwork the dough.
5. Divide the dough into 12 evenly sized balls, then place them in a pre-seasoned 12-inch cast-iron skillet or on a parchment-lined baking sheet.
6. Bake for 18 to 20 minutes, until the tops of the biscuits are golden brown and the center is cooked. Remove from the oven and let cool until the cast iron is safe to touch, or use a pair of tongs to remove the biscuits.
7. Serve warm.
8. These can be stored at room temperature in an airtight container for 2 to 3 days, or frozen in a freezer-safe container or bag for up to 3 months.

Chapter Three

SMALL BITES
and NIBBLES

FINGER FOOD AND SNACKS: THE REAL REASON WE SHOW UP FOR PARTIES

Nibbles that can be scooped with a chip, stuck on a stick, or plucked from a tray and popped straight into your mouth are a staple for gatherings. While you don't always have to make a main meal for a party, your guests always appreciate a few snacks. I myself will happily make a meal out of small bites and appetizers if given the chance. I've been known to order only from the appetizer menu at restaurants instead of having a main course. I have made, can make, and will continue to make a meal out of a bowl of Pico de Gallo (page 92) and tortilla chips.

And oh man, if you put food on a toothpick?

Guaranteed I will eat it.

Now you will understand why my Garlic and Brown Sugar Bacon Pineapple Bites on page 103 have the most adorable little drink umbrellas stuck in them—not only do they look cute, but I love a delicious bite-sized snack served up on a stick. No messy hands, it's discreet, and hardly anyone will notice if you eat three in a row—let's be honest, you just can't beat that.

From cheese balls to meatballs, deviled eggs to chicken wings, this chapter includes some recipes that are truly entertaining staples in my family. My mom doesn't go anywhere without taking her deviled eggs—and more often than not it's usually politely requested by the host that she bring a few dozen. However, the one small-bites recipe that I can truly claim has been the most requested above all else for baby showers, weddings, and the like is my mom's pinwheel sandwiches.

Today's tortilla-wrapped, cream cheese–stuffed pinwheel sandwiches make me wistful for the pinwheels of my childhood. Don't get me wrong, some of those are fantastic, but those aren't the *real* pinwheel sandwiches that I grew up with.

These sandwiches were served at every bridal shower, community hall party, and baby shower in my family for as long as I can remember. The most commonly asked question at any gathering of our friends and family was "Is your mom bringing her sandwiches?" So, for this book about cooking for parties, events, and gatherings, I knew that I would have to share her fillings recipes with all of you. It's a cliché to say, but these sandwiches honestly make people's eyes light up with delight when you bring them to a party.

It's Not a Party Without Pinwheel Sandwiches!

I'm fully aware of why modern pinwheel sandwiches have eschewed fresh bread and turned to tortilla wraps: the original pinwheel sandwiches are a lengthy labor of love that can take an entire afternoon or evening to make if you are doing various fillings. You have to order the bread from a bakery and have them slice it horizontally (lengthwise) and then go pick it up. You have to cut the edges off the ends and then carefully roll them up. Then you have to wait a day for everything to set before you slice and serve. But oh, my dear friends, it is worth it. It's also a family event; I can't count the times that my mom, sister, and I sat down together at a big table and filled and rolled and cut these sandwiches for someone's gathering.

It's not just fresh bakery bread that transforms pinwheels from great to amazing—it is the mayonnaise. And when I say mayonnaise, I mean full-fat mayo! While low-fat mayo has its place, it isn't for pinwheel sandwiches as it makes the sandwich filling watery and soggy—because remember, they had to replace the fat in the mayo with something!

We usually order one 1-pound rectangular loaf of bread for every batch of filling we make, which yields 6 rolls usually, though sometimes only 5. Your local store that has an in-store bakery will have its brand of white and whole-wheat loaves of bread that they will slice horizontally for you—and the loaves are almost always 1 pound. Don't worry if they are slightly larger, they will still work.

Each sandwich roll you fill and roll is then sliced into 6 or 7 slices, so if a batch of filling makes 6 rolls, you will end up with 36 to 42 round pinwheel sandwiches (6 rolls × 6 pieces per roll = 36 pinwheels). You can do the math to figure out how many batches and loaves of bread you need for your gathering.

To sum up: 1 pound loaf of horizontally sliced bread + 1 batch of filling = 6 sandwich rolls = 36 to 42 pinwheel sandwiches for your guests.

To create the rolls, we usually clear the entire table and sit down for the process—I suggest you do the same!

see over

Pinwheel Fillings

Here are the four recipes that we use without fail when making pinwheels. For all the recipes, there will be a yield of how many regular sandwiches the filling makes and how many pinwheel sandwiches they make as well, so you have a general idea of what to expect for both types.

MOM'S EGG SALAD SANDWICH FILLING

My mom isn't allowed to go home from a visit to my house without making me a batch of her egg salad filling. I then eat nothing but egg salad sandwiches for the next few days, which is enough to satisfy my cravings until Mom comes to visit again. I finally cajoled her into writing down her recipe for me and I was surprised at how quick and easy it is. She uses less mayo than most recipes, which I think is her secret as it allows the egg flavor to shine through. I honestly will choose my mom's egg salad sandwich over any other sandwich out there. For those of you who eschew bread, this egg salad is amazing on sliced cucumber for a gluten-free option.

Fills 8–9 regular sandwiches or 5–6 pinwheel sandwich rolls |
Prep Time: 5 minutes | Total Time: 5 minutes

12 hard-boiled eggs, cooled and peeled

½ cup mayonnaise

⅓ cup finely diced celery

¼ cup minced green onions, green and white parts

Salt and pepper

1. Place the eggs in a large mixing bowl. Using a large fork, mash the eggs into small chunks. The smaller the chunks, the smoother the egg salad. I prefer mine with some texture.
2. Mix in the mayo, celery, and green onions, then add salt and pepper to taste.
3. This will keep in an airtight container in the fridge for up to 4 days.

SALMON SANDWICH FILLING

One would think that a sandwich with fish and onion filling would be completely ignored at an event, but like all of the other pinwheel fillings, these salmon sandwiches are always popular. Just make sure to have other food options available so that your guests aren't looking for breath mints at the end of the day! (Or better still, have some breath mints ready!)

Fills 9–10 regular sandwiches or 5–6 pinwheel sandwich rolls |
Prep Time: 5 minutes | Total Time: 5 minutes

3 cans (7.5 oz/213 g each) well-drained salmon

½ cup mayonnaise

¼ cup minced green onions, green and white parts, or ¼ cup finely minced white onion

⅓ cup minced celery

Salt and pepper

1. Combine the salmon, mayo, onions, and celery in a large bowl. Add salt and pepper to taste.
2. You can make this 1 day ahead of time, but any longer and the quality will deteriorate.

CHICKEN SALAD SANDWICH FILLING

Pro tip: rotisserie chicken from the store makes the best chicken salad ever, and it's always the easiest way to get 4 cups of chicken. I generally get 4 cups from one store-bought chicken, so if you want to double this recipe, buy 2 chickens. We always use a mixture of white and dark meat, as Mom's chicken salad was always made with leftovers.

Fills 6–7 regular sandwiches or 5–6 pinwheel sandwich rolls |
Prep Time: 5 minutes | Total Time: 5 minutes

4 cups loosely packed chopped chicken

¾ cup mayonnaise

⅓ cup minced celery

¼ cup minced green onions, green and white parts

Salt and pepper

1. In a large bowl, combine the chicken, mayo, celery, and green onions. Add salt and pepper to taste.
2. Keep refrigerated until you use it. You can make this 1 day ahead of time, but any longer and the quality will deteriorate.

SPAM PINWHEEL SANDWICH FILLING

There is a certain generation that will love you—nay, they will absolutely *adore* you—for bringing them a Spam sandwich, so yes, I've included that recipe here as well, even though I personally don't understand the love for it. We always make one batch of this sandwich, and every time it disappears, much to my surprise!

Fills 6–7 regular sandwiches or 5–6 pinwheel sandwich rolls |
Prep Time: 5 minutes | Total Time: 5 minutes

1 can (12 oz/340 g) Spam or Klik

6–8 Tbsp mayonnaise

¼ cup sweet relish, drained of juice

Pepper

1. In a medium bowl, shred the canned meat with a fork, pulling it apart until it's light and fluffy.
2. Add the mayo, relish, and pepper, adjusting to taste if needed. (Sorry, yes, I am making you taste-test them. Taking one for the team, okay?)
3. Keep refrigerated until you use it. You can make this up to 2 days ahead of time, but any longer and the quality will deteriorate.

CREATING THE PINWHEEL SANDWICHES

1 roll aluminum foil

1 bread knife

1 butter knife

1 cutting board

1 lb salted butter

As many batches of sandwich filling as required

As many loaves of bread as required

6 dill pickle slices per sandwich-filling recipe, well drained and patted dry with paper towel

1. To create, take 1 slice of the bread and lay it on a cutting board. Butter the bread well, then remove the short crust ends with the bread knife. (If you butter it afterward the ends tear.) Spread one-sixth of the filling onto the bread. At the end nearest you, lay a pickle slice across the width. Roll up the sandwich starting at the pickle, making sure it's rolled just tightly enough to compress together but not squish the bread.
2. Take a sheet of aluminum foil and wrap up the roll tightly. Repeat until the filling is used up and you have 5 to 6 rolls. Repeat with all the fillings. Refrigerate overnight.
3. The next day, remove each roll from the foil. Slice the remaining crust ends off (they make a great snack before the party!) and slice into ½-inch-wide pinwheels. Place on serving platters and cover, keeping refrigerated until served.

Cream Cheese Pastry Dough

This simple and forgiving pastry is an often overlooked classic that can be used in savory and sweet dishes. This is great for the Brie Saskatoon Tartlets on the next page, but you can also use it to make 14 to 16 regular tart shells and try them with my Classic Canadian Butter Tarts on page 172! This recipe also makes a very forgiving and easy pie crust for a large 10-inch pie.

Makes one 10-inch double pie crust, 16 regular tarts, or 36 tartlets | Prep Time: 10 minutes | Total Time: 1 hour, 10 minutes

1 cup butter, softened

1 package (8 oz/226 g) cream cheese, softened

2 cups all-purpose flour

½ tsp salt

1. In the bowl of a stand mixer fitted with the paddle attachment, beat the butter and cream cheese together until completely smooth. Add the flour and salt, mixing on low speed until a smooth dough forms.

2. Form into a disk and cover with plastic wrap. Chill for at least 1 hour. This can also be made ahead of time with excellent results.

3. Because of the cream cheese, the dough shouldn't be frozen, but can remain in your fridge for up to 5 days.

Brie Saskatoon Tartlets

I wanted to come up with an easy, homemade appetizer that really spoke to the Prairies—and included my love of hot, melty Brie. There's nothing like a burst of berry flavor in the middle of winter to help chase away the blues. And melty cheese never hurts.

Makes 3 dozen tartlets | Prep Time: 30 minutes | Total Time: 1 hour, 50 minutes

Saskatoon Sauce

2 cups fresh or frozen saskatoon berries

1 cup water

½ cup white sugar

3 Tbsp cornstarch

1 Tbsp lemon juice

Tartlets

1 batch Cream Cheese Pastry Dough (page 85)

16 oz double cream Brie cheese, chopped into 36 small pieces

Fresh or defrosted frozen saskatoon berries, for topping (optional)

◆ ◆ ◆

Refrigerate any leftover Saskatoon berry sauce filling for 3 to 4 days and enjoy on ice cream or toast!

◆ ◆ ◆

1. Preheat the oven to 350°F.
2. To make the sauce, in a medium-sized stockpot, place the saskatoon berries, ¾ cup of the water, and the sugar. Bring to a slow boil over medium-high heat and simmer for 10 to 11 minutes, until the berries have softened.
3. Whisk the cornstarch into the remaining ¼ cup water and then rapidly whisk into the pot. Stir in the lemon juice and cook for another 2 to 3 minutes until the sauce thickens. You want the filling to resemble thick pie filling, keeping in mind the mixture will thicken as it cools. If needed, mix another cornstarch slurry consisting of 3 tablespoons cornstarch and ¼ cup water, then whisk in 1 tablespoon of the mixture at a time, cooking after each addition, until thickened, remove from the heat and set aside to cool.
4. To make the tartlets, on a lightly floured work surface, roll out the cream cheese pastry ⅛ inch thick. Using a 3-inch round cookie cutter, cut out 36 circles. Press the circles into lightly greased mini muffin tins by gently using the round end of a wooden spoon, forming a shell.
5. Place 1 to 2 tablespoons of the saskatoon berry sauce in each cup, filling them almost to the top.
6. Bake for 17 to 20 minutes, until the pastry is golden brown. Remove from the oven, turn the oven off, and place a piece of Brie on top of each tartlet. If wanted, place a whole saskatoon berry on top for garnish.
7. Return to the still-warm oven for 1 to 2 minutes, to just melt the cheese. Remove and let cool until just warm, then serve.
8. These can be stored at room temperature in an airtight container for 2 to 3 days, or frozen in a freezer-safe container or bag for up to 3 months.

Donna's Deviled Eggs

Deviled eggs used to be something you enjoyed on the down low; you really didn't want anyone knowing that you still ate them. Let's face it, we associated them with tables full of jellied aspics and crazy canned meat concoctions of the 1970s. Nowadays, thanks to chefs bringing their gussied-up versions onto their appetizer menus in droves, deviled eggs are back in fashion. It astounds me how fast my deviled eggs disappear whenever I bring them to a function and how people rave about how much they love them. They probably devour them because the recipe is actually my mom's! Why is it that recipes by our moms are always so much better?! So here you are: MY mom's recipe for delicious deviled eggs!

Makes 2 dozen egg halves | Prep Time: 15 minutes | Total Time: 15 minutes

12 large eggs, hard-boiled, cooled, peeled, and rinsed

½ cup full-fat mayonnaise

1 tsp mustard

½ tsp Worcestershire sauce

1–2 Tbsp very finely minced green onion, green part only (optional)

Salt and pepper

Regular paprika for sprinkling (optional)

1. Slice each egg in half lengthwise. Carefully remove the egg yolks without ripping a hole in the whites and place in a medium-sized bowl.
2. Arrange the egg whites on a serving platter in one layer.
3. Using a fork, mix the mayo, mustard, Worcestershire sauce, and onion (if desired) into the egg yolks, combining until creamy and smooth. Add salt and pepper to taste.
4. Using either a pastry bag or a plastic bag with a large star-shaped piping tip attached, pipe the egg yolk mixture back into each egg white, filling to just over the top. Each egg should have a small dome of filling.
5. Sprinkle with paprika if desired. Keep cold until serving.
6. These are best eaten the same day, but can be stored in an airtight container in the fridge for 1 to 2 days. They will get watery if kept too long.

VARIATIONS

Curried: add ½ teaspoon of mild curry powder to the mayo mixture; garnish with a sprinkle if desired.

Smoky bacon: sprinkle with smoked paprika instead and garnish with bits of crumbled cooked bacon. Try an applewood or hickory smoked bacon for variations.

Relish lovers': add 2 tablespoons of sweet relish to the mayo mixture.

Dill pickle: add 2 tablespoons of finely chopped dill pickles and 1 teaspoon of dried dill to the mayo mixture. Garnish with extra dill.

Classic Cereal Snack Mix

This recipe, often known as Nuts and Bolts, is THE quintessential Canadian Christmas party snack; however, I make them regularly throughout the year for parties as this mix can take the heat and isn't perishable in the sun. This recipe is cheaper and so much tastier than all the store-bought party mixes and will conjure up fond childhood memories for most of us. We like ours heavy on the garlic (that whole Ukrainian thing; you can't escape it) so I use the full 3 tablespoons of garlic powder in mine.

You can also substitute in other items such as Cheezies at a 1:1 ratio: remove 1 cup of cereal from the original recipe, then add in 1 cup of the substitution. As for additional spices, simply add them to the mixture!

Makes 22–24 cups of mix | Prep Time: 5 minutes |
Total Time: 1 hour 30 minutes to 2 hours

The Basics

8 cups Crispix cereal (plain corn and rice)

4 cups plain Rice Chex

4 cups plain Cheerios

4 cups pretzel sticks

1 box (7 oz/200 g) cheese stick crackers (Cheese Bits)

2 cups salted butter

2–3 Tbsp garlic powder

1 Tbsp seasoning salt

1 Tbsp paprika

½ Tbsp onion powder

3 Tbsp Worcestershire sauce

Optional Butter Sauce Additions

½ Tbsp dried dill, added to the butter mixture

1 Tbsp Sriracha, buffalo sauce, or chili sauce

1. Preheat the oven to 250°F.
2. In a very large roasting pan, combine the cereals, pretzels, and crackers. Chose 1 to 2 cups of dry ingredient additions from the list if desired, and add to the mixture.
3. In the microwave (or on the stove), melt the butter and mix in the spices and Worcestershire. Add the optional butter sauce ingredients at this point if desired. Pour the butter mixture over the dry ingredients and stir gently to mix thoroughly. You want to coat everything in the butter mixture, but not break up the ingredients.
4. Bake for about 1½ to 2 hours, stirring gently with a spoon every 30 minutes or so.
5. The mix will be done when you can see that all the butter mixture has been absorbed and the pieces of the mix are dry. This is a forgiving recipe and shouldn't burn easily, but if you see pieces getting too dark too early, lower your oven temperature to 200°F and let the mixture dry out at a lower temperature for another hour or so, still stirring every 25 to 30 minutes.
6. Remove and cool completely in the pan, and then store in an airtight container. This can be frozen in sealed plastic bags for up to 3 weeks or kept in sealed containers at room temperature for up to 5 days.

Optional Dry Ingredient Additions

2 cups cheesy goldfish-shaped crackers (great for kids' parties!)

1 cup crumbled cooked bacon

2 cups Shreddies

1 cup unsalted roasted peanuts

2 cups hard cheese-flavored puffs (aka Cheezies— the kind you can only get in Canada)

2 cups soft cheese-flavored puffs (available everywhere)

Pico de Gallo

Sometimes I am seriously lazy. I'll admit it. There are a few items that I'm more fond of eating than making, and pico de gallo is one of them. The chopping everything into small pieces, the gloves required for the jalapeño (please don't touch jalapeños or any other hot pepper without using food-grade plastic gloves, you guys!) . . . everything just leads up to the fact that I don't want to make it, I just want to eat it. Luckily for you, none of the stores in my area make pico de gallo, so I was forced to learn how to make it myself—and yes, this is far better than any store-bought version! This is an incredibly versatile snack that you can easily tweak to your liking. You can customize the heat level with the amount of jalapeño pepper, add garlic, and, of course, play around with the lime level.

Makes 4–5 cups, depending on size of tomatoes used |
Prep Time: 25 minutes | Total Time: 1 hour, 25 minutes

6 large Roma tomatoes

1 Tbsp sea salt

1 cup very finely diced red onion

¾ cup loosely packed chopped cilantro

3 Tbsp minced garlic

2 Tbsp minced jalapeño pepper (½–1 pepper)

¼ cup lime juice (about 2 medium limes)

Sea salt and pepper

Tortilla chips, for serving

1. Chop the tomatoes into small cubes and place them in a colander over a large bowl or your sink. Sprinkle with the sea salt, toss, then leave to drain for 15 minutes, tossing every 5 minutes or so until you have removed a large amount of liquid and the seeds.

2. Combine the drained tomatoes, red onion, cilantro, garlic, jalapeño, and lime juice in a large bowl, mixing until combined, and season to taste with salt and pepper.

3. Cover with plastic wrap and refrigerate for 1 hour to let the flavors meld, then serve with tortilla chips.

4. The pico de gallo will keep for 2 days in an airtight container in the refrigerator, but is best eaten within a few hours as it gets watery.

Tips

> *To prep the jalapeños, wear food-grade plastic gloves. Slice the jalapeños in half and remove the seeds and the white membrane inside with a spoon. Dice into very small pieces—the smaller they are, the better spread out the flavor and heat will be in your pico de gallo.*

> *If you find raw onions too sharp-tasting in dishes, soak the diced onions in water for 20 minutes, and then drain.*

✦ ✦ ✦

Real French Onion Soup Dip

I took one of my favorite soups, French Onion, and turned it into a hot dip for a fresh new update to the 1970s classic, the onion soup mix dip. Maybe it's because of our Prairie climate, which is chilly for eight months of the year, but a cheesy, hot dip on an appetizer table is pretty much a requirement. Swirling those bread cubes around until you have loaded them up with hot dip, then popping them into your mouth, delivers a cheesy, carb-loaded bite of heaven. For a traditional taste, use Gruyère, but mozzarella is also amazing.

Makes 12–15 servings | Prep Time: 60 minutes | Total Time: 1 hour, 20 minutes

4 cups thinly sliced yellow onions

¼ cup salted butter

2 tsp minced garlic

⅓ cup dry red wine

⅓ cup strong beef broth made from powdered bouillon

½ tsp dried thyme leaves

1 package (8 oz/226 g) cream cheese, softened

¼ cup sour cream

½ cup shredded Gruyère

1 cup shredded mozzarella, divided

1 tsp pepper

1 large round sourdough loaf

Crackers for serving: seedy, sturdy crackers are the best for this heavy dip

1. Preheat the oven to 325°F.
2. Place the onions and butter in a large skillet. Fry the onions on medium heat until they are soft and brown (caramelized) for 30 to 40 minutes. Add the garlic and sauté until lightly browned, 2 to 3 minutes.
3. Add the red wine, broth, and thyme. Simmer for 4 to 5 minutes, reducing until there is almost no liquid left.
4. Combine the cream cheese and sour cream in a mixing bowl, and mix until smooth with an electric mixer. Stir in the onion mixture, the Gruyère cheese, and ½ cup of the mozzarella until completely incorporated.
5. Take the sourdough loaf and cut a circle in the top, leaving a ½-inch rim of bread around the top edges and cutting two-thirds of the way down into the loaf. Remove the bread circle carefully, as you'll use it for dipping. Cut the removed bread into cubes and store in an airtight bag until serving time.
6. Spoon the dip into the sourdough bread bowl until it's full. Place on a baking tray and top with the remaining ½ cup of shredded mozzarella. Bake for 20 to 25 minutes, until the dip is heated through and the cheese has melted on top.
7. Remove and allow to cool for a few minutes, then serve immediately with the cubed bread and crackers.
8. Depending on your guests, you'll either discard the bread bowl once done or the entire thing will get eaten!

2-for-1 Dill Pickle Dip

This is a 2-for-1 dilly of a dip. If you stop at the point right before you add the pickles and juice, you simply have a fabulous dill dip—one of my favorite dips ever. If you add the pickles, you've moved into dill pickle dip territory. It is extremely customizable—my dad would double or triple the garlic, of course—to suit your taste. It is also better if it sits overnight, with the pickles added the next day, but if you are in a pinch for time, it's a great dip made a few hours beforehand.

Pair this with my Dill Monkey Bread (page 72) for the perfect appetizer for dill lovers!

Makes 2½ cups | Prep Time: 15 minutes | Total Time: 15 minutes, plus overnight chilling

BASIC DILL DIP

1 package (8 oz/226 g) cream cheese, softened

1 cup sour cream

2 Tbsp mayonnaise

1½ tsp garlic powder

½ tsp onion powder

⅓ cup chopped fresh dill, or 3 Tbsp dried dill

Salt to taste

DILL PICKLE VERSION

1½ cups finely chopped dill pickles

1 Tbsp dill pickle juice, or to taste

1. Place the cream cheese, sour cream, and mayonnaise in a medium-sized bowl. Using an electric mixer, combine thoroughly, until the cream cheese is incorporated and not lumpy.
2. On low speed, mix in the garlic powder, onion powder, dill, and salt. Cover and refrigerate overnight or for 2 to 3 hours in the fridge if pressed for time.
3. To make dill pickle dip, add the chopped dill pickles and pickle juice just before serving.
4. Serve with vegetables, crackers, in a bread bowl . . . the sky is the limit! This does not store well once you add the pickles, so use it within 24 hours after adding them.

Sweet and Sour Meatballs

These meatballs are one of the very first things to disappear at parties, no matter how many I make. I've tested their popularity again on my relatives at the family reunion, and an entire pot of these vanished before anything else, including the perogies—at a party full of Ukrainians!

This recipe is a two-part family affair: my mom makes incredible meatballs, and I have perfected the sauce.

Makes 4–5 dozen meatballs | Prep Time: 20 minutes |
Total Time: 1 hour, 10 minutes to 1 hour, 20 minutes in oven
or 8 hours, 20 minutes to 10 hours 20 minutes in slowcooker

Mom's Meatballs

4 lb lean ground beef

2 eggs

1 cup seasoned dried bread crumbs

¼ cup grated white onion (optional)

2 Tbsp garlic puree (found in a tube in the fresh grocery section)

2 Tbsp Worcestershire sauce

½ Tbsp salt

½ tsp pepper

Karlynn's Sweet and Sour Sauce

2 cups packed brown sugar

6 Tbsp all-purpose flour or cornstarch

3 cups water

½ cup white vinegar

½ cup ketchup

6 Tbsp light soy sauce

1. Preheat the oven to 375°F or set out a slow cooker.
2. To make the meatballs, place all the meatball ingredients in the bowl of a stand mixer fitted with the paddle attachment. Mix until everything is well combined. Form 1½-inch-wide meatballs and place them on rimmed baking sheets, half an inch apart, until the meat mixture has been used up.
3. Bake for 20 minutes. Transfer the meatballs to a 13- to 15-inch roaster or a slow cooker, shaking off any grease first.
4. To make the sauce, combine all the sauce ingredients in a large saucepan. Bring to a boil over medium-high heat, whisking constantly to prevent lumps from forming. Once the sauce thickens enough to coat the back of a spoon, remove the pan from the heat.
5. Pour the sauce over the meatballs.
6. If using the oven, bake for 30 to 40 minutes, or until the meatballs reach an inside temperature of 165°F.
7. If using a slow cooker, cook on low for 8 to 10 hours, until the meatballs reach a temperature of 165°F. Serve hot—a slow cooker will keep these warm throughout a party.
8. These can be stored, sauce and all, in the refrigerator in an airtight container for 2 to 3 days, or frozen in a freezer-safe container or bag for up to 3 months.

Salt and Pepper (Chili) Chicken Wings

Once upon a time there was an old hotel (fittingly named the Old Hotel) in Airdrie, Alberta. This hotel wasn't the type of place a 20-year-old girl would regularly hang out, but on Wings Night my parents, siblings, Mike, and I would head down there for 10-cent wings and listen to the small-town bands playing. They made the best salt and pepper wings I have ever eaten. While that hotel is long gone now, the memory of those amazing wings remains. This recipe is as close as I will ever get to indulging in those wings again, at my home, without deep-frying.

Makes 3 dozen wings | Prep Time: 10 to 15 minutes | Total Time: 40 to 45 minutes

BASIC SALT AND PEPPER WINGS

4 tsp finely ground black pepper

2 tsp large-flake sea salt

1 tsp table salt

1–2 Tbsp vegetable oil

3 lb party wings (about 36 wings)

CHILI SALT AND PEPPER COATING (OPTIONAL)

4 tsp toasted sesame oil

2 Tbsp minced garlic

¼ cup minced green onion, green and white parts

1 tsp red chili flakes (optional)

1. Preheat the oven to 450°F.
2. Whisk the pepper and both salts together in a small bowl. Break up any large sea salt flakes with the back of a spoon—you want them medium-sized for an extra salty crunch. If you prefer a finer salt all over the wings, use a total of 3 teaspoons of table salt instead of the table salt and sea salt mix.
3. Lightly oil a large baking tray with the vegetable oil, then spread the chicken wings on it in one layer. Sprinkle the wings with the salt and pepper, then shake the baking tray to cover the wings completely, turning them to coat as needed.
4. Bake for 10 to 15 minutes, then turn and bake for another 15 to 20 minutes, until crispy and cooked through. Do not undercook—you want to crisp up the wings. If you want basic salt and pepper wings, stop here and serve them as is.
5. To add the optional chili coating, place the wings in a large bowl.
6. Heat the sesame oil in a small skillet over medium heat. Add the garlic and sauté until light brown and fragrant, then add the green onions and, if you want an extra kick, chili flakes. Fry for another minute, then pour the oil over the chicken wings in the bowl. Toss, coating the wings completely with the mixture.
7. Serve and enjoy!
8. These wings will last in an airtight container in the fridge for 2 to 3 days but will not reheat well. They are delicious eaten cold as leftovers!

Garlic and Brown Sugar Bacon Pineapple Bites

I couldn't do a section on nibbly, bite-sized food without wrapping something in bacon, right? I made these on a cold, miserable rainy day, and with the first tentative, taste-testing bite I immediately wanted to throw a retro luau or tiki-themed party just so that I could make these as an appetizer. The garlic and brown sugar sauce is a staple on green bean and asparagus bundles that are wrapped in bacon, but when I was trying to think of something new for an appetizer, my mind went to fruit. Mr. Kitchen Magpie doesn't even like pineapple generally, but he ate three of these in the blink of an eye. I have a feeling that this recipe will convert many people to eating delicious savory pineapple dishes!

Makes 30 bites | Prep Time: 20 minutes | Total Time: 40 to 45 minutes

15 slices bacon (about 1 lb)
2 fresh medium-sized pineapples
1 cup packed brown sugar
2 tsp garlic powder

1. Preheat the oven to 375°F. Line a baking tray with parchment paper.
2. Slice the bacon slices in half widthwise, creating 30 pieces.
3. Peel the pineapples and cut off the tops and bottoms. Slice each pineapple into 5 thick rings. Take out the core of each ring, then slice each ring into 6 pieces.
4. Mix the brown sugar and garlic powder together, then spread the mixture onto a large plate.
5. Dredge the bacon slices in the sugar mixture, coating both sides. Wrap each slice around a pineapple chunk and secure it with a toothpick. Place on the prepared rimmed baking tray.
6. Bake for 20 to 25 minutes, until the bacon is crispy. Remove and serve hot. If desired, replace the toothpicks with drink parasols as shown in the photo.
7. Serve immediately.

Carol's Cheese Ball

This recipe dates way back to the 1970s, when my parents lived in Lockport, Manitoba. My mom's good friend and neighbor shared her cheese ball recipe with my mom—and it's the only one that we have used for every holiday gathering and party ever since. I have yet to meet anyone who doesn't loves a good cheese ball and crackers—especially one with bacon—except for Mr. Kitchen Magpie. That is, until he tried this cheese ball. I think it's because this is a nut-free version, which is so good that it might just convert the non–cheese ball lovers!

Serves 8–10 people (or 1 Mr. Kitchen Magpie) | Prep Time: 10 minutes | Total Time: 12+ hours

1 lb old cheddar, grated

1 package (8 oz/226 g) cream cheese, softened

1 can (4.25 oz/120 g) deviled ham

¼ cup finely chopped green onion, green and white parts

2 tsp mustard

½ tsp salt

½ tsp celery seed

8–10 slices hickory bacon, cooked crisp, blotted of grease, and crumbled

1. In a large mixing bowl, using a wooden spoon, mix together the cheddar, cream cheese, ham, green onions, mustard, salt, and celery seed until well combined. Use your hands to form into a ball.

2. Place the crumbled bacon on a large dinner plate, and then roll the ball in the bacon crumbles, coating evenly and completely.

3. Wrap in plastic wrap and refrigerate overnight.

4. Serve with crackers or even celery sticks for scooping. The wrapped cheese ball will last in the refrigerator for 4 to 5 days and will freeze exceptionally well for up to 2 months when wrapped in aluminum foil overtop of the plastic wrap.

♦ ♦ ♦

Cheese Ball Tip

You can also roll this into 2 balls like we do: one for my husband and one for the rest of us. No word of a lie: my mom makes him his own cheese ball at Christmas. Simply make more crumbled bacon to coat them both.

♦ ♦ ♦

OH, THOSE VEGGIES

Truth time: I loathe most salads. Salads remind me of dieting in high school—and oh my word, speaking of high school can I please have my Grade 12 body back? PLEASE? I won't complain about it this time, I promise! The other mental block I have with salads is that the mere thought of a salad can bring forth the image of tasteless wilted greens that are the starter for most chain restaurants. There, I said it. You're the cheapest therapy there is!

Here's another secret: Sometimes it's hard to make a vegetable dish that everyone will enjoy. Especially my husband, Mr. Kitchen Magpie, who is the non-vegetable-eating bane of my existence. That man will live on meat and potatoes (can you tell he's Irish or what?) and could go for weeks on end without touching anything green or orange. And I get it. Salads are almost always the last thing remaining on the tables at events unless they are of the mayonnaise-based variety—and don't you worry, I have those in this chapter. But I also wanted to come up with three winning healthy salads that will get everyone, including Mr. Kitchen Magpie, to give salads a chance.

You will notice that not a single salad in this section uses iceberg lettuce or romaine. I love the peppery snap of arugula and also using fruit in all my salads as it satisfies my sweet tooth and makes salads so much more interesting to eat—like my Mango, Avocado, and Arugula Salad (page 112), which Mr. Kitchen Magpie now enjoys, or my Dragon Fruit, Apple, and Arugula Salad (page 113).

I finally have convinced Mr. Kitchen Magpie to eat cabbage too. Sure, he had a change of heart when I wrapped cabbage in bacon in my Bacon-Wrapped Cabbage Wedges (page 111): that sure convinced him that he should stop avoiding it. This chapter also pairs sweet potatoes with curry, chipotle, and honey to make a dish that will impress those who thought they didn't like sweet potatoes—or curry. I baked parsnip into a casserole. I even stuffed things into tomatoes. The stuffed tomatoes were the first vegetable that I have ever seen Mike eat after supper was over. He did the "I'm cleaning dishes and will also snack over the sink while packing up leftovers, even though I just ate supper" bit with those tomatoes.

If I had to pick the one recipe I use the most in this entire cookbook, it would be the Slow-Cooker Molasses "Baked" Beans on page 121 in this chapter. Knowing a fantastic slow-cooker bean recipe has eliminated the need to ever open another store-bought can of molasses beans again.

While it was a challenge to get some of these recipes just right for those picky eaters, we now have some new family favorites that we enjoy on a regular basis. I hope you find some new favorites too!

Dragon Fruit, Apple, and Arugula Salad (page 113)

Bacon-Wrapped Cabbage Wedges

This is the recipe that convinced Mr. Kitchen Magpie that he liked eating cabbage instead of just tolerating it. Sure, he ate coleslaw when I made it for lunch, but this recipe? He will purposely pick up a cabbage now when he's grocery shopping so that he can make this. And make it he does. He has mastered this recipe and makes it every couple of weeks for us. This is probably the only cabbage recipe that I'd ever serve at a dinner party, because bacon and cheese makes everything better!

Makes 4–6 servings | Prep Time: 20 minutes |
Total Time: 1 hour, 5 minutes to 1 hour, 20 minutes

1 small green cabbage

12–18 slices applewood or hickory smoked bacon, depending on cabbage size

½ cup mix of grated Parmesan and Asiago cheese

1. Preheat the oven to 350°F. Line a rimmed baking tray with parchment paper.
2. Peel off and discard the outer leaves of the cabbage. Cut the cabbage in half from the top through to the core at the bottom. Cut one cabbage half into 4 to 6 wedges from top to bottom again, without cutting the cores out of the wedges (you need the core so the leaves don't fall apart). The wedges have to be narrower than your bacon is long, so that you can wrap the bacon around them. Wrap the remaining cabbage half in plastic wrap and refrigerate to use later, perhaps in my Tropical Coleslaw recipe coming up on page 117.
3. Take 3 slices of bacon and coat each in the shredded cheese, coating each side. Lay the 3 strips side by side on the baking sheet. Place a cabbage wedge in the middle of the bacon, perpendicular to the bacon slices. Take both ends of a bacon slice, fold them into the center of the cabbage wedge, and then secure in place with a toothpick, sticking it through the bacon and into the cabbage.
4. Repeat for all the cabbage wedges.
5. Bake for 45 to 60 minutes, until the cabbage has softened all the way to the middle. Test by piercing with a knife: if the knife goes easily to the middle of the cabbage, it's ready.
6. Serve immediately.

Mango, Avocado, and Arugula Salad

I could have called this "Use Up The Fruit That's Going to Go Bad in My Fruit Bowl Salad," because that's exactly how and why this salad came to be. I looked at the expensive mangos that my son always wants me to buy and then forgets to eat, and then I looked at the also expensive avocados that I always buy and forget about and got cranky enough to make a salad with them. This salad goes well with both vinaigrette recipes below.

Makes 4–6 servings | Prep Time: 20 minutes | Total Time: 20 minutes

SALAD

8–10 cups arugula

3 mangos, peeled and sliced

3 avocados, peeled and cubed

½ cup very finely diced red onion

MISO VINAIGRETTE

¼ cup rice vinegar

3 Tbsp toasted sesame oil

3 Tbsp honey or agave nectar

2 Tbsp canola oil (or other neutral-flavored oil)

2 Tbsp white miso

1½ Tbsp soy sauce

1–2 Tbsp lime or lemon juice (about 1 medium lemon or lime)

1-inch piece of fresh ginger, peeled

Black or white sesame seeds, for garnish (optional)

RASPBERRY VINAIGRETTE

¼ cup olive oil

3 Tbsp lime juice (about 2 medium limes), or to taste

1 Tbsp raspberry balsamic vinegar

1–2 tsp honey, or to taste

Salt and pepper to taste

1. For the salad, in a large bowl, gently toss together the arugula, mangos, avocados, and red onions.
2. To make the miso vinaigrette, place all the ingredients except the sesame seeds in a food processor and blend until smooth. Adjust the sweetness or acidity as desired.
3. To make the raspberry vinaigrette, place all the ingredients in a lidded jar and shake until combined. Adjust the sweetness or acidity as desired.
4. Drizzle your vinaigrette of choice over the salad, coating well. Serve immediately.
5. Any extra dressing can be stored in a sealed container in the fridge for up to a week.

Dragon Fruit, Apple, and Arugula Salad

My kids love dragon fruit, and I'm sure it's because of the name. Nevertheless, dragon fruit are readily available at your local grocery store and their mild taste pairs perfectly with almost any ingredient you can think of, even feta cheese like in this salad. My advice for serving this at a party is to make it into a salad bar. Keep all the ingredients separate and let guests build their salad with the arugula, fruits, walnuts, and feta. This recipe as written makes 2 lunch-sized salads or small side salads for 4 to 6 people.

Makes 4–6 servings as a side or 2 as a main | Prep Time: 15 minutes

Salad

6–8 cups arugula

1 large dragon fruit, peeled and sliced

2 apples, washed, cored, and sliced

½ cup toasted walnuts

⅓ cup feta cheese, crumbled

Citrus Dressing

½ cup olive oil

2 Tbsp melted honey

2 Tbsp lemon juice

1 tsp mustard

1 tsp poppy seeds

½ tsp salt, or to taste

1. For the salad, place the arugula leaves on a large platter. Top with the dragon fruit, apple, walnuts, and feta.
2. For the citrus dressing, place all the ingredients in a lidded jar and shake to combine. Adjust the honey and salt to taste.
3. Drizzle the dressing over the salad.
4. Serve with a set of salad tongs so people can help themselves. Alternatively, you can set out the salad ingredients individually and make a build-your-own-salad bar.
5. Any extra dressing can be stored in a sealed container in the fridge for up to a week.

Minty Feta, Cherry, and Watermelon Salad

This was my favorite salad of summer '17. My son and I ate . . . and ate . . . and ate this until we couldn't even look a watermelon in the eye. It's a riff on one of my favorite salads at Disney World—the very salad that convinced me that mint, feta, and watermelon are a match made in heaven. As always, a fruit salad means a juicy salad, so make sure to let the watermelon drain for 20 minutes or so before you add anything to it. If you like, toss a few cups of arugula in with this as well to get your greens in.

Makes 4–6 servings | Prep Time: 20 minutes | Total Time: 20 minutes

MINT HONEY DRESSING

¼ cup liquid clover or flower honey

2 Tbsp lime juice (about 1 medium lime)

1 Tbsp water

5 fresh mint leaves

SALAD

6 cups ¾-inch cubes of seeded watermelon, drained well in a colander

1½ cups pitted and halved cherries

½ cup fresh mint leaf chiffonade

½ cup crumbled feta cheese

1. To make the dressing, in a 4-cup-capacity microwave-safe measuring cup, mix together the honey, lime juice, and water. Crush the mint leaves with the end of a wooden spoon to release the oils, but leave them intact, and then add to the mixture.

2. Microwave on high for 2 to 3 minutes, until the mixture is bubbling. Remove the mint leaves and set the dressing aside to cool.

3. To make the salad, in a large bowl, mix together the watermelon, cherries, and mint.

4. Once the dressing has cooled, pour it over the watermelon mixture and toss gently to coat. Sprinkle with feta cheese and serve immediately.

5. The salad does not store well, but the dressing can be kept in a sealed container in the refrigerator for 2 to 3 days.

Tropical Coleslaw

Although the recipes on my website are mainly for meals and desserts, I do eat salads in real life, usually for lunch, when I remind myself that I should eat vegetables more often. You'll still rarely catch me eating iceberg lettuce; this salad was whipped up when I had too much cabbage left over from making Bacon-Wrapped Cabbage Wedges (page 111). That's the thing: when you have a large head of cabbage in the kitchen, it seems to keep going endlessly sometimes. This is a wonderful way to use it up!

Makes 6–8 servings | Prep Time: 25 minutes | Total Time: 25 minutes

Coleslaw

8 cups shredded green and purple cabbage (bagged mixes work great)

2 cups fresh or 20 oz canned pineapple chunks, drained on paper towel

1 cup grated carrots, rinsed well with cold water to remove starch

1 large mango, peeled and cut into ½-inch cubes, drained on paper towel

⅓–½ cup chopped cilantro

Chili Lime Dressing

2 Tbsp lime juice (about 1 medium lime)

2 Tbsp lemon juice (about 1 medium lemon)

½ cup olive oil

2 Tbsp honey

1 tsp chili powder

½ tsp salt

1. To make the coleslaw, in a large bowl, toss the cabbage, pineapple, carrots, mango, and cilantro together.
2. To make the dressing, place all the ingredients in a lidded jar and shake until combined.
3. Drizzle the dressing over the salad in the bowl; toss to coat.
4. Serve immediately. The dressing may be stored in a sealed container in the refrigerator for up to a week, but the salad itself does not keep well.

◆ ◆ ◆

Salad Tips

➤ Carrots can add an undesirable starchy "mouth feel" to a salad when mixed with acidic dressings and fruit. Make sure to rinse or soak them in cold water after you chop or grate them to remove the starch.

➤ When you use fruit in a salad, cut and lay the pieces on paper towel to absorb some of the juice. Salads containing fruit are best made close to when you're going to eat them.

◆ ◆ ◆

Retro Picnic Macaroni Salad

There is nothing that says "summertime picnic" like an excellent macaroni salad. This recipe has been my family's go-to for as long as I can remember. You can cut this recipe in half for smaller gatherings if you wish. You can also substitute elbow macaroni, but I have found that the twisted tortiglioni pasta holds its shape better than the traditional elbow macaroni does. There is nothing more retro than a salad with a sugar, mayo, and pickle juice dressing!

Makes 16 servings | Prep Time: 30 minutes | Total Time: 3 hours, 30 minutes

MACARONI SALAD

1 (1.1 lb/500 g) package tortiglioni (twisted, curled hollow tube pasta)

1¼ cups small cubes of old cheddar cheese

1 cup diced bread and butter pickles

2 cups frozen peas

10 green onions, green part only, finely chopped

1 lb hickory smoked bacon, cooked until crispy, cooled, and chopped (or 1 cup diced cooked ham)

4 eggs, hard-boiled and roughly chopped

RANCH MAYONNAISE SALAD DRESSING

1 package (1 oz/28 g) dry ranch salad dressing mix

1 cup full-fat mayonnaise

½ cup grated Parmesan cheese

3 Tbsp white sugar

¼ cup bread and butter pickle juice

2 Tbsp mustard

1 tsp seasoning salt

1. To make the salad, cook the pasta according to the package directions for al dente pasta. Drain, run under cool water until cold, drain again, and place in a large bowl.

2. Add the rest of the salad ingredients to the bowl and mix thoroughly.

3. To make the dressing, place all the dressing ingredients in a lidded jar and shake to combine.

4. Pour the dressing over the salad; stir to coat the salad entirely with the dressing.

5. Refrigerate until serving. This salad is best if left a few hours in the fridge or even overnight so that the flavors meld together. This salad can be stored in an airtight container for up to 2 days in the refrigerator.

Mom's Potato Salad

When, at one point in my 20s, I first asked my mom to write down her potato salad recipe, two things happened. One, she told me that she had never written it down, she just makes it from taste (which is true of all of the cooks in my family, except me—I went and got a job blabbing recipes to the world at large). Two, once I finally coerced her to measure the ingredients and write them down for me, I accused her of hiding a secret ingredient from me, telling her that there was no way that this list of simple ingredients made my favorite potato salad! However, it does and I'm convinced that it's some type of sorcery. (I've actually figured out that it's because she loads it up with more eggs than anyone else I know, and it makes it a combination of potato salad and egg salad that to me is perfection—but I still tell her it's sorcery.)

Makes 6–8 servings or 1 bowl for me to eat for 3 days straight |
Prep Time: 30 minutes | Total Time: 7 hours, 50 minutes

3 lb medium yellow, waxy potatoes like russet or Yukon Gold, peeled and quartered

10 hard-boiled eggs, coarsely chopped

½ cup finely diced celery

½ cup chopped or sliced radishes, your preference

4 green onions, green and white parts, finely chopped

2 cups mayonnaise

2 tsp mustard

Salt and pepper

Extra chopped green onions or smoked paprika, for garnish (optional)

1. Place the potatoes in a large stockpot and pour enough water over top to cover them. Bring to a boil over high heat, stirring occasionally.

2. Turn down the heat to medium-high and boil for 20 to 25 minutes, until the potatoes are fork-tender but not falling apart.

3. Remove from the heat and drain into a colander. Cool for 10 to 12 minutes.

4. Once the potatoes are cool enough to handle, cut them into ½-inch cubes.

5. Transfer the potatoes to a large mixing bowl. Add the eggs, celery, radishes, and green onions.

6. In a small bowl, combine the mayonnaise and mustard. Scoop over the salad ingredients. Gently stir the mayo mixture into the vegetables until everything is coated completely and mixed. Add salt and pepper to taste and garnish if desired.

7. Cover with plastic wrap and refrigerate for 3 to 4 hours before serving.

8. This will store, covered, in the refrigerator for 2 to 3 days.

Slow-Cooker Molasses "Baked" Beans

There is nothing like a pot of homemade baked beans to get the party started! (You can take that any way you want. Beans, beans, the magical fruit . . .) Truly, though, every time I am at a potluck and someone brings a slow cooker full of their homemade beans, they are the person being pestered for their recipe constantly throughout the event. Homemade baked beans may take a while to make, but it's a seriously *easy* while. Soak them overnight. Then you literally throw all the ingredients into a slow cooker, let them cook them all day or overnight, and you're done. This is a large recipe meant for a crowd, and it's perfect for freezing into batches for dinners later—make sure to save some for my Calico Beans (page 156).

Makes 16 servings | Prep Time: 10 hours | Total Time: 20 hours, including soaking and cooking

4 cups dried navy beans

1 lb old-fashioned thick-sliced bacon

1 cup finely diced white onion

1½ cups ketchup

½ cup fancy molasses

¾ cup packed brown sugar

3 Tbsp Worcestershire sauce

1 Tbsp mustard

1 tsp salt

½ tsp black pepper

Pinch of ground cloves

3–4 bay leaves

4 cups boiled hot water

1. Place the beans in a large stockpot or bowl and cover with water. Soak overnight, then drain the beans and place them in your slow cooker.

2. Slice the bacon crosswise into short strips. Add the bacon and onion to the slow cooker.

3. In a medium-sized saucepan, mix together the ketchup, molasses, brown sugar, Worcestershire sauce, mustard, salt, pepper, and cloves. Bring to a boil over medium-high heat, stirring frequently, then pour over the bean mixture in the slow cooker.

4. Stir the mixture, then add the bay leaves. Pour the hot water over top, making sure that the beans are completely covered. Stir again to mix, then place the lid on the slow cooker and cook for 8 to 10 hours on low. Start testing for doneness at the 8-hour point. The beans are done when they reach the desired texture and softness.

5. These are even better the next day after the flavors meld together, so they can be prepared ahead of time. Simply refrigerate and then reheat the next day. These can be stored in the fridge in an airtight container for 2 to 3 days, or frozen in a freezer-safe container for up to 3 months.

Stuffed Florentine Tomatoes

The first time I made these stuffed tomatoes, they ended up being the main course instead of an appetizer. Everybody ignored the soup and the salad I made, and we all ate these instead. I also might have caught Mr. Kitchen Magpie eating one over the sink after supper as an extra "snack" immediately after dinner. To make them as a main course, simply use six to eight 3- to 4-inch-wide on-the-vine tomatoes and increase the cooking time by another 15 to 20 minutes. They must be cooked to an internal temperature of 165°F because of the eggs.

Makes 2 dozen tomatoes | Prep Time: 30 minutes |
Total Time: 1 hour, 5 minutes to 1 hour, 10 minutes

Tomatoes

24 cocktail tomatoes (1½–2 inches wide)

Salt

Sausage Filling

1 package (12 oz/375 g) ground mild or spicy Italian sausage

1 cup finely diced white onion

1 tsp minced garlic

1 package (10 oz/283 g) frozen chopped spinach, defrosted and squeezed of excess moisture

½ cup dry Italian-seasoned bread crumbs

2 eggs, beaten

¾ cup grated Parmesan cheese

½ tsp salt

Twenty-four 1½-inch squares of mozzarella cheese

chopped fresh flat-leaf parsley, sea salt, and pepper, for garnish (optional)

1. Preheat the oven to 350°F. Place a 10- × 16-inch wire rack on a 12½- × 18½-inch baking tray (or any wire rack that fits into your baking trays will do).

2. To prepare the tomatoes, carefully slice off the top of each one. Using a teaspoon, carefully scoop out the insides until the cavity is clear. Discard the tops and the insides. Sprinkle a little salt in each tomato shell and then place upside down on the prepared wire rack to drain.

3. To make the filling, in a large skillet over medium-high heat, sauté the Italian sausage and onion until the sausage has cooked through and the onion is soft and translucent. Add the garlic and cook for another minute. Drain any excess fat.

4. Add the spinach and fry for 3 to 4 minutes to get rid of any excess moisture. Transfer the contents to a large mixing bowl to cool.

5. Once the mixture is cool to the touch, mix in the bread crumbs, eggs, Parmesan cheese, and salt.

6. Stuff each tomato with the filling just to the top, then place it upright on the rack. If it doesn't stand up, you can slice off a small part of the tomato bottom to make it flat.

7. Bake for 30 to 35 minutes or until the filling reaches a minimum temperature of 165°F. Top each tomato with a slice of mozzarella cheese, then return to the oven. Bake until the cheese has melted.

8. Serve hot. These can be stored in the fridge in an airtight container or wrapped in plastic wrap for 2 to 3 days, but they are best when eaten fresh.

Curried Honey Chipotle Sweet Potatoes

Curry and honey go together like Thor and Chris Hemsworth: you simply can't have one without the other. Add some butter, mustard, and sweet potatoes and you have the easiest side dish that will win you rave reviews at any party! This dish is a perfect example of how you don't need 15 to 20 ingredients to make a dish that is truly pectacular. Err, I mean spectacular. Sorry, I got distracted for a moment dreaming about Chris Hemsworth. The chipotle powder in this was a happy accident. I didn't have any of the red pepper flakes that I usually like to sprinkle on for heat and tried chipotle instead, and now I'll never go back!

Makes 6–8 servings | Prep Time: 10 minutes | Total Time: 50 to 55 minutes

10 cups sweet potatoes, peeled and diced into ½-inch cubes

2 Tbsp olive oil

1 tsp salt

½ cup melted butter

½ cup honey

¼ cup mustard

1 tsp curry powder (you can use mild or spicy, as you desire)

¼ tsp chipotle chili pepper, plus extra for seasoning

1. Preheat the oven to 350°F.
2. In a medium-sized bowl, toss the sweet potatoes with the oil and salt until completely and evenly coated. Place on a baking tray and bake for 20 minutes, stirring at the 10-minute mark, until the potatoes start to soften.
3. Whisk together the butter, honey, mustard, curry powder, and chipotle, then pour over top of the sweet potatoes, coating thoroughly.
4. Continue baking for another 20 to 25 minutes, stirring occasionally, until the potatoes are fork-tender.
5. Remove and serve hot. Sprinkle with salt and more chipotle powder to taste.
6. This can be stored in an airtight container for 2 to 3 days in the refrigerator.

Dill and Onion Scalloped Potatoes

Every early summer, my family and I cook up what we consider traditional simple Ukrainian fare; a simple potato dish made with new potatoes, cream, and fresh dill. There is simply nothing like this combo of flavors first thing in the summer with new potatoes fresh from your own garden—to me, that taste means summer has officially arrived. I've taken those beloved flavors and made them into a more complex scalloped potato dish.

Makes 6–8 servings | Prep Time: 30 minutes | Total Time: 2 hours, 20 minutes

4 Tbsp salted butter, divided

3 lb russet or Yukon Gold potatoes, skin on

2 cups finely diced white onion

2 Tbsp minced garlic

2 cups milk

1 cup whipping cream

¼ cup cornstarch

½ cup chopped fresh dill, or ¼ cup dried dill

1 tsp salt

¼ tsp pepper

2 cups grated Swiss cheese, divided

½ cup grated Parmesan cheese

1. Preheat the oven to 350°F.
2. Using 2 tablespoons of the butter, grease a 9- × 13-inch glass or ceramic baking dish or large casserole of comparable size.
3. Slice the potatoes into ¼-inch-thick slices, leaving the skin on if you prefer and just giving them a good scrub. (I do this with fresh garden potatoes.)
4. In a large skillet over medium-high heat, sauté the onion in the remaining 2 tablespoons butter until softened, about 15 minutes. Add the garlic and sauté for another 2 to 3 minutes, or until the garlic is browned and fragrant.
5. In a measuring cup, mix together the milk and cream, then whisk in the cornstarch until smooth. Pour this into the skillet, stirring constantly while pouring. Stir in the dill, salt, and pepper. Bring to a simmer and continue to simmer for 3 to 4 minutes, until thickened, adjusting the salt, pepper, and dill to taste. Remove from the heat.
6. Place half the potatoes in a fairly even layer in the bottom of the baking dish. Overlapping potatoes are OK. Pour half the milk mixture over top, then sprinkle on 1 cup of the Swiss cheese. Place the remaining potatoes on top in another layer and pour the remainder of the milk mixture over them. Cover loosely with aluminum foil.
7. Bake for about 1½ hours, until fork-tender, checking for doneness after 1¼ hours. Remove the foil and top with the remainder of the Swiss cheese and all of the Parmesan cheese. Bake for another 15 to 20 minutes, until the cheese is brown and bubbly.
8. Let cool for 10 minutes before serving.

Parsnip Bake

If you don't like parsnips, turn the page now, please. This recipe is for lovers of parsnip, that underappreciated underdog root vegetable that grows so incredibly well in our Prairie climate. This is a dish that embraces the sweet tones of the parsnip instead of going savory. You also have two options: take out the egg for a creamier, more mashed-potato-like filling, or keep the eggs for a firmer casserole that you can cut into squares easily, as shown in the photo. Choose your own parsnip adventure!

Makes 6–8 servings | Prep Time: 20 minutes |
Total Time: 1 hour, 10 minutes to 1 hour, 20 minutes

PARSNIPS

2 lb parsnips

¼ cup melted butter

2 Tbsp honey

1½ tsp salt

⅛ tsp ground nutmeg

2 eggs, beaten (optional)

½ cup all-purpose flour

1 tsp baking powder

HONEY PANKO TOPPING

¾ cup panko breadcrumbs

2 Tbsp melted butter

1 Tbsp honey

¼ tsp salt

1. Grease a 9- × 9-inch baking pan with butter.
2. To make the parsnips, peel and slice them into ½-inch-thick rounds. Place in a large saucepan and cover with warm water. Bring to a boil over high heat and continue to cook on a low boil until the parsnips are tender and falling apart, around 15 minutes. Drain well in a colander.
3. Place the parsnips in a large mixing bowl and mash with a potato masher or potato ricer until they are smooth.
4. Mix in the butter, honey, salt, and nutmeg. Taste-test at this point and add more salt if needed.
5. Mix in the eggs completely, if you are using them.
6. Whisk together the flour and baking powder, then mix into the parsnips.
7. Preheat the oven to 350°F.
8. Place the mashed parsnips in the prepared pan and smooth them out in an even layer.
9. Bake uncovered in the oven for 30 minutes.
10. To make the topping, mix the topping ingredients together in a small bowl. Taste-test to see if you need to add more salt.
11. Remove the pan from the oven and sprinkle the topping over the parsnips in an even layer.
12. Return to the oven and bake for another 15 to 20 minutes, until the topping has browned.
13. Let cool for a few minutes before serving.
14. This can be stored in an airtight container for 2 to 3 days in the refrigerator.

Make-Ahead Loaded Mashed Potato Casserole

I love a good mashed potato bake, and I also love to load things up. These baked mashed potatoes have everything but the kitchen sink on top, including potato chips! Double the potato carbs, double the deliciousness! Make sure not to skip them, as the chips are what make this side dish a hit with their crunchy goodness. Make-ahead mashed potatoes are one of the best ways you can save time—instead of spending time prepping this dish on the day of your dinner or event, you can make these the day before and free up that time day of for something else. That said, these can also be made the same day and baked right away.

Makes 10 servings | Prep Time: 30 minutes |
Total Time: 1 hour, 10 minutes to 1 hour, 20 minutes

4 lb potatoes (russet or Yukon Gold), peeled and cubed

½ cup butter, cubed

4 oz cream cheese, cubed, room temperature

½ cup sour cream

¼ cup heavy cream

1 tsp onion powder

1 tsp seasoning salt

1 tsp garlic powder

½ tsp pepper

2 cups shredded medium or old cheddar cheese

½ cup chopped green onions, green part only

8 slices hickory smoked bacon, cooked until crisp, then crumbled

½ cup crumbled plain potato chips

1. Grease a 9- × 13-inch glass or ceramic baking dish.
2. Place the potatoes in a large pot and cover with water. Bring to a boil and cook until the potatoes fall apart when pierced with a fork, 20 to 25 minutes. Drain the potatoes, then return them to the pot.
3. Using a potato masher, mash the potatoes with the butter, cream cheese, sour cream, heavy cream, onion powder, seasoning salt, garlic powder, and pepper until smooth with few lumps.
4. Spread the potato mixture in the prepared dish in an even layer. Sprinkle the cheese, onions, bacon, and potato chips on top. Cover with plastic wrap and refrigerate until the next day. If you are in a hurry, these can be made right away.
5. When ready to bake, preheat the oven to 350°F.
6. Cover the baking dish with aluminum foil and bake for 35 to 40 minutes. Remove the foil and bake another 5 to 10 minutes, until the topping browns and crisps up. Serve.
7. This can be stored in the refrigerator in an airtight container or wrapped in plastic wrap for 2 to 3 days.

Buttery Mushroom Rice

cheater!

This is my favorite rice dish. It also happens to use my favorite canned soup. I can eat this as a meal, but it also makes for an amazing side dish. No one will guess how easy it is to make, and although leftovers are amazing reheated the next day, I rarely have any—and I bet you won't be able to resist a second helping either. Carbs, butter, and mushroom soup—my comfort food trifecta!

Makes 8–10 servings | Prep Time: 5 minutes | Total Time: 55 minutes to 1 hour

2 cups long-grain white rice

2 cans (10½ oz/284 mL each) condensed mushroom soup

2¼ cups beef broth

1 cup salted butter

1. Preheat the oven to 425°F.
2. Grease a 9- × 13-inch glass or ceramic baking dish with butter.
3. Mix the rice, soup, and broth together, then pour mixture into the prepared baking dish.
4. Cut the butter into thin slices and place randomly on top of the mixture.
5. Cover with aluminum foil, or a lid, and bake for 30 minutes. Remove the cover and bake for 20 to 25 minutes more. The rice is ready when it's soft and fluffs up with a fork nicely.
6. This can be stored in an airtight container for 2 to 3 days in the refrigerator.

Bacon, Walnut, and Honey Brussels Sprouts

This recipe is how I get Mr. Kitchen Magpie to eat his vegetables. No word of a lie, he's worse than my kids. I will cut him some slack, however, as the microwave-steamed Brussels sprouts that we ate while we were growing up pale in comparison to the delicious Brussels sprouts dishes of today. The best part of these are the little leaves that fall off and turn into crispy little sprouts chips.

Makes 4–6 servings | Prep Time: 5 minutes | Total Time: 25 minutes

2 slices bacon, diced

25–30 medium-sized Brussels sprouts, washed, trimmed, and halved

½ cup walnuts

2 Tbsp melted honey

Salt and pepper

1. In a large skillet, fry the bacon over medium heat until it starts to shrivel up and starts to release its grease, 3 to 4 minutes. Swirl the bacon around to coat the pan with the released grease.

2. Add the Brussels sprouts, laying them cut side down in the pan in one layer to start. Fry them until they get browned and crisp, 5 to 7 minutes, then turn them over. Continue to cook until tender-crisp when pierced with a fork.

3. Add the walnuts and fry for 4 to 5 minutes, until they are toasted.

4. Remove from the heat and drizzle the melted honey over the top, tossing until the honey coats everything evenly. Sprinkle with salt and pepper to taste.

5. Serve and enjoy.

6. These can be stored in an airtight container in the refrigerator for 2 to 3 days.

◆ ◆ ◆

To add some heat, sprinkle red chili flakes into the dish.
Sweet + heat = perfection!

◆ ◆ ◆

Chapter Five

MAIN DISHES

THE MAIN EVENT

I can't honestly remember the last time I held a sit-down or ever a semi-sit-down dinner at my house. I have thrown a few over the years, but I always found that being in the kitchen cooking while my company visited with my husband wasn't the best way to catch up on the latest news or to pay my guests attention. We slowly switched over from having couples' dinners to larger, informal gatherings where we load up the slow cooker and the bar with serve-it-yourself options. And instead of hovering in the kitchen all night, you can chat with your guests and (my particular favorite) sit down to a table of game-play. We've even held parties where every table—and the kitchen island—were covered in board games, with groups of people huddled around in (friendly) competitive play. Lately, theme parties have also taken place, where guests come dressed up and we choose the food to fit the theme.

At a *Mad Men* party we threw, we set up the kitchen counter with a slow cooker full of hot, from-scratch Chicken à la King and had the kitchen table loaded up and groaning under the weight of 1960s fare such as Donna's Deviled Eggs (page 88), Carol's Cheese Ball (pineapple-shaped!) (page 104), and, of course, Classic Cereal Snack Mix (page 90). Almost everything was prepped or made ahead of time, so I was able to sit and visit with my guests.

When you're holding a lengthy part that goes late into the night, there comes a time in the evening when everyone is ready for a hearty dish, a main dish. The main dishes in this chapter are what you are going to fill up your guests with—and let's face it, the main meal will help soak up the Mr. Kitchen Magpie's Old-Fashioneds (page 251) that they have been drinking as well. Most of the main meals in this chapter are protein-loaded and stay warm perfectly in a slow cooker. A few are vegetarian options should you want those as well, like my Yellow Curry Slow-Cooker Cauliflower, Chickpeas, and Vegetables (page 157) or Gnocchi Pesto Caprese Salad (page 164). Many of the slow-cooker versions can also be made on the stove top.

As with all the recipes in this book, the recipes in this chapter double for dinners at home or as dinners to go. These dishes are easy to make, serve, and/or transport and are surefire crowd-pleasers.

Happy entertaining!

Yellow Curry Slow-Cooker Cauliflower, Chickpeas, and Vegetables (page 175)

Hawaiian Pizza Bun Sliders

Did you know that the inventor of the Hawaiian pizza was a Canadian? As a Canadian myself, I find it very fitting that the sliders I chose for this cookbook are ones that mimic my favorite pizza. You can make all sorts of sliders with buns; however, these sliders use my Hawaiian Sweet Buns (page 60) and a delicious buttery topping that pairs sweet with garlic. You really do need sweet buns to make this easy dinner perfect! If you are short on time, you can use store-bought buns, just make sure they are a sweet roll.

The key to this recipe is to keep the batch of 12 buns together when removing them from the pan that they are baked in, then slicing the buns horizontally without separating them. You'll then end up with one complete layer of bun tops and one layer of bun bottoms.

Makes 1 dozen sliders | Prep Time: 10 minutes, plus Hawaiian Sweet Buns |
Total Time: 40 to 45 minutes, plus Hawaiian Sweet Buns

BASIC HAWAIIAN PIZZA

12 Hawaiian Sweet Buns (page 60), still together in their 9- × 13-inch baked form

¾ cup pizza sauce

12 thin slices cooked ham

1 can (14 fl oz/398 mL) pineapple chunks, well drained (reserve 2 Tbsp juice)

2 cups shredded pizza mozzarella

TOPPING (OPTIONAL)

¼ cup melted salted butter

¼ tsp garlic powder

1 tsp brown sugar, or to taste

1 tsp poppy seeds

1. Preheat the oven to 375°F.
2. Slice the 12 buns horizontally to remove the tops from the bottoms, leaving all the top halves attached and all the bottom halves attached so that you have 2 complete layers. Place the bottom layer of buns in a glass or ceramic 9- × 13-inch dish. Pour the pizza sauce over this layer of buns and spread it evenly. Place the ham slices on top, slightly overlapping, then sprinkle the pineapple chunks on top. Spread the shredded cheese on top of the pineapple in an even layer, and then place the top layer of buns on top of it all.
3. If you want to use the topping, whisk together the melted butter, reserved pineapple juice, garlic powder, sugar, and poppy seeds. Brush this mixture over the tops of the buns.
4. Cover the buns with aluminum foil and bake for 30 to 35 minutes, until the buns are heated through and the cheese has melted.
5. Slice into individual sliders while still in the pan, making sure to cut all the way through the layers.
6. Serve hot. These do not store well, so are best eaten the same day.

Chicken à la King

This isn't your open-a-can-of-soup Chicken à la King, my friends. I made this for a *Mad Men* soiree a few Christmases ago, and it was scarfed up faster than you can say "Betty Draper." While I don't mind a good can of soup recipe (see page 29, for example), I had a house full of food industry friends and wasn't about to pull out the cans of soup for them. I also wanted to make a version that tasted nothing like the 1960s version, but rather something you might find on a restaurant menu. This will stay hot in your slow cooker all evening long on the cooker's "keep warm" setting.

Makes 24 servings | Prep Time: 25 minutes |
Total Time: 1 hour, 20 minutes on the stove top or 9 hours in slow cooker

¼ cup butter

1 cup finely diced white onion

2 cups sliced button mushrooms

2 cups diced carrot

1 Tbsp minced garlic

5 cups strong chicken stock, made from powdered bouillon

¼ cup dry white wine

½ tsp celery salt

1 tsp dried thyme leaves

1 cup heavy cream

¼ cup cornstarch

5–6 cups cooked chicken breast, chopped into bite-sized pieces

1 cup fresh or frozen baby green peas

⅓ cup chopped jarred pimentos

Salt and pepper

24 puff pastry vol-au-vent shells (found in the freezer section of grocery stores)

◆ ◆ ◆

Cooked celery in a slow-cooker dish never ends up toothsome. A dash of celery salt adds the flavor without the mush.

◆ ◆ ◆

1. In a large frying pan over medium-high heat, melt the butter and sauté the onion, mushrooms, and carrot, until the onions are soft, around 15 minutes. Add the garlic and cook for another 2 to 3 minutes or until the garlic is fragrant.

2. Mix in the chicken stock, wine, celery salt, and thyme. To cook in the slow cooker, cook on low for 8 hours. To cook on the stove top, cook in a large stockpot and bring to a low simmer. Cover and cook on medium heat for 45 minutes.

3. For the slow cooker, an hour before you are ready to eat, whisk together the cream and cornstarch. Whisk into the slow cooker, stirring rapidly to ensure there are no lumps. Mix in the chicken, peas, and pimentos. Cook for another 60 minutes, stirring every 20 minutes.

4. For the stove top method, 10 minutes before you are ready to eat, whisk together the cream and cornstarch. Whisk the mixture into the soup, stirring rapidly to ensure there are no lumps. Mix in the chicken, peas, and pimentos. Cover and simmer on low for another 10 minutes.

5. Bake the puff pastry shells according to package directions. Remove the pre-cut centers and set them aside.

6. To serve, pour a ladleful of the sauce onto the pastry, then place the reserved pastry center overtop the sauce.

7. Any leftover sauce can be kept in an airtight container in the refrigerator for 2 to 3 days.

Grandma Ellen's Cold Picnic Barbecue Fried Chicken

My mind was completely blown when my friend Kandice casually mentioned that her Grandma Ellen used the same potato-chip fried chicken recipe that I did, but used barbecue chips instead of plain chips and served it cold as can be. It was a favorite family picnic fare, and since it was served cold, you could have fried chicken from the cooler any time you wanted. She admitted that she had never eaten this chicken warm, and funnily enough, I always made my fried chicken and served it hot for dinner, so I can tell you that it's an amazing hot meal as well. Having said that, if there is one thing in this world I love to eat for breakfast, it's cold fried chicken.

Seriously. Coffee and cold fried chicken: the breakfast of champions.

Makes 8 pieces | Prep Time: 10 minutes | Total Time: 1 hour, 20 minutes, including chilling

3 eggs

1⅓ cups all-purpose flour

2 cups crushed barbecue potato chips

⅓ cup margarine (use one that has vegetable oil, to raise the smoke point for high-heat cooking) or butter

8 pieces of chicken, skin on, bone in. This recipe will coat up to 8 breast pieces, so you can mix and match smaller pieces of chicken accordingly.

1. Grease a rimmed baking tray large enough to hold 8 pieces of chicken in a single layer and set aside.
2. Beat the eggs in a bowl just large enough to hold the largest piece of chicken. Place the flour and crushed chips in 2 separate bowls.
3. Line up your bowls and your baking tray in this order from left to right: flour, eggs, crushed chips, baking tray.
4. First, dip your chicken into the flour mixture and cover it completely and evenly. Shake off any excess flour.
5. Dip it into the egg mixture, shaking off any excess, and then into the crushed chips, rolling it around to cover it completely. Place the piece of chicken on the baking tray, and repeat with the remaining chicken.
6. Place in the fridge for 30 minutes minimum and up to 1 hour.
7. Preheat the oven to 400°F.
8. Melt the margarine and drizzle it evenly over the chicken pieces.
9. Bake uncovered for 40 to 50 minutes, or until the chicken reaches 165°F for breast meat and 180°F for dark meat. If you are using butter, check periodically to make sure that it's not smoking; if it does, turn down the oven temperature.
10. Serve warm or refrigerate immediately if using for a picnic.

Rum 'n' Cola Glazed Picnic Ham

It's time to picnic like a pirate! There is nothing easier and more versatile to feed a crowd of people with than a big picnic ham. You can serve it hot or cold, slice it, put it in sandwiches . . . The options are almost endless when it comes to this classic. I've mixed old and new—a retro pineapple-and-maraschino-topped ham with a newfangled garlic, spiced rum, and cola glaze that would make the captain himself proud.

On a side note, while I say that hams take 20 minutes a pound, which is the standard, mine never heat that fast. My mom and I are always arguing about when to put the ham in the oven—and we never get it right. Luckily, hams are very forgiving if you allow yourself extra time.

Makes 10–12 servings | Prep Time: 10 minutes | Total Time: 2 to 3 hours

½ cup spiced rum

1 can (12 oz/355 mL) cola

½ cup packed brown sugar

2 Tbsp minced garlic

½ cup honey

1 can (8 oz/227 g) pineapple rings in juice, drained

One 5–7 lb bone-in pork shoulder picnic ham, precooked, all wrapping removed

½ cup Maraschino cherries, soaked overnight in enough rum to cover

1. Whisk together the rum, cola, sugar, garlic, and honey. Place the pineapple rings in the mixture to marinate while the ham is cooking.

2. Preheat the oven to 275°F. Place 2 very large pieces of aluminum foil crosswise (they should be long enough to wrap over the ham) in the bottom of a large roasting pan.

3. Place the ham cut side down on the foil. Bring the edges of the foil up around the ham and scrunch them together to tent it. Heat the ham for 20 minutes per pound or until the center of the ham is warmed to 135°F. Fold back the foil and score the ham fat in a crosshatch pattern.

4. Brush some of the rum mixture over the top of the scored ham, making sure to get into all the nooks and crannies. Fix the pineapple rings to the ham, using a large toothpick and a cherry (see photo) for each one. Baste everything again, including the cherries and pineapple rings, and return to the oven uncovered. Heat for another 20 to 40 minutes, brushing the ham with glaze every 10 minutes or so, until the ham has reached a minimum temperature of 140°F.

5. Slice and serve.

6. The ham can be stored in an airtight container for 2 to 3 days in the refrigerator.

The Best Homemade Beef Hamburgers

Sometimes the best recipes are the simplest ones, and while I know I proclaimed my reluctance to label anything the "best," I am going to make an exception here. After countless hours of reading on the Internet, taking some of the information and discarding numerous things I determined were simply myths (like not using bacon), I came up with what I consider to be the perfect hamburger recipe. I also came up with the best way to form your burger patties. One of the keys to this recipe is to use fresh ground beef. Freezing ground beef will inevitably compress the meat, and as you will learn in the instructions, it's all about keeping the beef loose and light. I actually went to the local butcher and asked them to make me a few packs of it right in front of me. I do not recommend using lean or extra-lean beef, as the final burgers tend to come out too dry.

Makes 6 burgers | Prep Time: 15 minutes | Total Time: 15 to 20 minutes

2 lbs regular ground beef

1 tsp onion powder

3 slices bacon, diced small

½ cup shredded old cheddar cheese

1 egg, beaten

◆ ◆ ◆

I cook my patties on soapstone slabs on my barbecue because I find that they do a good job of keeping the juices in the meat (and preventing the flames from charring the burgers). You can find these online and at most barbecue retailers.

◆ ◆ ◆

1. Pull the ground beef loosely apart in a large bowl. You want to be gentle enough that the ground beef remains loosely packed, otherwise the juices won't spread through the burger properly. Once you've loosened up the beef, add the other ingredients and loosely mix with your fingers, just enough to combine.

2. To make the patties, form the ground beef mixture into a log. Cut the log lengthwise into 6 evenly sized pieces. I find that ⅓ pound is the ideal size for a burger once cooked.

3. To form the patty, use a 4-inch (28 oz/796 mL) can, opened at both ends with a can opener. Place a patty in the can and press down lightly with a round potato masher until the patty is shaped in a nice circle. Remove the can and place the patty on a plate for the barbecue. Repeat for all patties, and you've got perfectly formed, loosely packed patties ready to go!

4. Cook on the barbecue, or pan-fry, until the center reaches 165°F.

Turkey Taco Potato Skillet

Hello, perfect summertime picnic skillet! I came up with this skillet while we were glamping (I don't camp) one summer and knew immediately that it was cookbook worthy. Kids and adults alike scarfed it back and asked for seconds. It's easy, it uses homemade taco seasoning (another must-have), and you can substitute ground beef or chicken for turkey. A time-saving tip: make the ground meat mixture ahead of time and simply reheat with the potatoes in the skillet and serve.

Makes 4–6 servings | Prep Time: 10 minutes | Total Time: 45 minutes

Homemade Taco Seasoning

¼ cup chili powder

3 tsp ground cumin

2 tsp garlic powder

1 tsp onion powder

2 tsp paprika

2 tsp dried oregano leaves

½ tsp red pepper flakes

1 Tbsp salt

1 tsp pepper

1 Tbsp cornstarch

Taco Skillet

3 Tbsp olive oil

2 lb skin-on baby red potatoes, boiled until tender, cooled, and halved

1 lb ground turkey

2 cups shredded Tex-Mex cheese

1–2 avocados, diced

1 tomato, diced

¼ cup chopped cilantro

1. To make the taco seasoning, whisk together all the ingredients and set aside. This can be stored in a sealed container in your pantry for up to a year.
2. To make the taco skillet, place the olive oil in a large skillet and heat over medium-high heat. Fry the potatoes until they are hot and start to crisp slightly, then remove from the heat.
3. In a smaller skillet, fry the ground turkey over medium-high heat until it is no longer pink, 8 to 10 minutes. Drain off the grease. Add 3 tablespoons of the taco seasoning and then ¼ cup of water. Mix these into the ground turkey and fry for another 2 to 3 minutes. Transfer this mixture to the larger skillet with the potatoes.
4. On medium-high heat, fry the potatoes and the meat mixture together for 2 to 3 minutes. Remove from the heat and sprinkle the cheese on top. Scatter the avocado, tomato, and cilantro over top.
5. Serve with sour cream, salsa, or my Pico de Gallo (page 92).

Slow-Cooker Tropical Pork Fajitas

When it comes to parties, slow-cooker meals that stay hot and allow guests to dish up their meals at their leisure are my favorite. Like every recipe in this chapter, this pulled pork also makes a great dinner for your family, with plenty of leftovers for school and work lunches the next day. Make hot, fresh pork fajitas for dinner and then have cold tropical pulled pork sandwiches for lunch the next day. It's perfect!

Makes 8–10 servings | Prep Time: 20 minutes | Total Time: 6 to 8 hours, 20 minutes

1 Tbsp vegetable oil

3–4 lb pork shoulder roast

3 cloves garlic, minced

2 cups pineapple juice

¾ cup packed brown sugar

⅓ cup soy sauce

½ cup ketchup

¼ cup rice vinegar

1–2 Tbsp Sriracha

1 tsp freshly grated ginger

1 tsp chili powder

Salt and pepper

2 Tbsp cornstarch

Corn tortillas or buns

Topping suggestions: diced pineapple, mango chunks, chopped cilantro, shredded jicama, lime juice

1. Heat the oil in a large frying pan over medium-high heat. Sear the roast on all sides and then place in the slow cooker.

2. Whisk together the garlic, pineapple juice, brown sugar, soy sauce, ketchup, rice vinegar, Sriracha, ginger, chili powder, and salt and pepper to taste. Reserve 2 cups and pour the remainder over the roast. Place the reserved marinade in an airtight container and refrigerate. Cook the roast on low for 6 to 8 hours, until it shreds easily with forks.

3. When the roast is done, whisk the cornstarch into the reserved sauce and pour the mixture into a saucepan. Bring to a slow boil over medium-high heat, stirring continuously until the sauce thickens, 8 to 10 minutes.

4. Remove the pork from the slow cooker, place on a large platter, and shred with 2 forks. Pour the thickened sauce over the shredded pork, mixing it in completely.

5. Serve in the tortillas or buns with your desired toppings. This can be stored in an airtight container for 2 to 3 days in the refrigerator.

Slow-Cooker Beef Dips

I made a huge slow cooker full of beef for beef dips at our Big Ukrainian Party on the Prairie (see page 4), and they were a hit. There is nothing like a pot of tender, juicy beef that allows everyone to customize their sandwiches. Most of the kids ate their buns with plain meat, and most of the adults loaded theirs with Swiss cheese and the mushroom onion topping. It's a surefire crowd-pleaser every time.

Makes 10–14 servings | Prep Time: 20 minutes |
Total Time: 8 hours, 20 minutes to 10 hours, 20 minutes

Beef Dip

One 5 lb chuck or blade roast, strings removed

4 cups strong beef broth, made from powdered bouillon

⅓ cup soy sauce

2 Tbsp grated white onion, or 1 tsp onion powder

1 tsp dried rosemary

1 tsp dried oregano

½ Tbsp minced garlic

Buns of your choice

Toppings

2 Tbsp salted butter

2 cups sliced button mushrooms

1 white onion, cut into half rings

Swiss or provolone cheese slices, 1 per sandwich served

1. To make the beef, place the beef roast in the slow cooker.
2. Whisk together the broth, soy sauce, onion, rosemary, oregano, and garlic. Pour over the roast. Cook on low for 8 to 10 hours, until the roast shreds easily with forks.
3. Remove the beef and shred on a plate. Skim the fat off the top of the cooking liquid, strain (if desired), and return the beef to the pot.
4. To make the toppings, when you are ready to serve, place the butter, mushrooms, and onions in a medium-sized frying pan. Fry over medium-high heat until the onions are soft, about 15 minutes. Place in a serving bowl with a spoon for guests to help themselves.
5. Slice the buns in half and set out the cheese. Use tongs to serve the beef, and a ladle to serve up the cooking liquid into small bowls for dipping.

Slow-Cooker Macaroni Cheeseburger Soup

This crazy concoction of mine has been one of the most popular soup recipes on my website for years upon years now. It's something I just came up with on the spur of the moment one night, and it quickly became a company staple in my house. If you come to visit me for a weekend in the winter, I will make you this soup, guaranteed. It's hearty, delicious, and a kid-pleaser.

Makes 8–10 servings | Prep Time: 20 minutes |
Total Time: 1 hour on stovetop or up to 8 hours in slow cooker

1½ lb lean ground beef

1 small white onion, chopped

3 cloves garlic, minced

6 cups strong chicken stock

1 cup grated carrots

1 tsp dried basil

1½ cups macaroni noodles

1½ cups whole milk

8–16 oz cubed Velveeta cheese

1. In a large skillet, fry the ground beef until slightly browned, then add the onions and fry until translucent and soft.

2. Add the garlic and fry for 1 or 2 minutes, until light brown and fragrant. Place the ground beef mixture into a large stockpot or slow cooker. Pour the chicken stock over the beef mixture and then add the carrots and basil.

3. If you are making this on the stove top, simmer for 30 to 40 minutes. If using a slow cooker, cook on low for 6 to 8 hours.

4. Half an hour before you are ready to serve, add the macaroni. Cook until soft.

5. Whisk in the milk and Velveeta. Start with 8 ounces of Velveeta and then add more if it's not rich enough for your taste. Stir until the cheese is melted throughout the soup completely and the soup has heated back up.

6. This can be stored in an airtight container for 2 to 3 days in the refrigerator, or frozen in a freezer-safe container for up to 3 months.

Smoky Spanish Chickpeas and Rice

Yes, I made a vegan dish that is also gluten-free—and it's amazing! I whipped this up for my sister-in-law when she was eliminating meat, gluten, and dairy from her diet, and the entire family ate it happily. The real star in this is the smoked paprika, which is one of my favorite spices. This is my go-to dish when I have someone coming to my house with dietary restrictions because, with all those amazing flavors, no one will even notice it's vegan and gluten-free.

Makes 6 servings | Prep Time: 15 minutes | Total Time: 45 to 50 minutes

2 to 3 Tbsp olive oil

1 medium yellow onion, peeled and diced finely

3 cloves garlic, minced

1 Tbsp smoked paprika

1 Tbsp dried oregano leaves

1 cup long-grain white rice, rinsed

1 can (19 fl oz/540 mL) diced tomatoes

2 cans (19 fl oz/540 mL each) chickpeas, drained and rinsed well

1½ cups gluten-free vegetable broth

¾ tsp salt

Chopped flat-leaf parsley, for garnish

1. Place the olive oil in a large skillet that has a lid (also known as a sauté pan). Heat the oil over medium-high heat and then add the onions and fry until soft and translucent, 6 to 7 minutes.
2. Add the garlic, fry for 2 to 3 minutes, then add the paprika and oregano. Fry for 1 to 2 minutes.
3. Add the rice and fry for 2 to 3 minutes.
4. Add the tomatoes with their juice, the chickpeas, vegetable broth, and salt.
5. Stir until the all ingredients are dispersed evenly throughout the skillet.
6. Bring to a simmer, then reduce the heat to medium and place the lid on top.
7. Simmer for 20 to 22 minutes, then remove the skillet from the heat—with the lid still on—and let sit for 5 or 6 minutes.
8. Remove the lid, fluff the rice, and top with chopped parsley to serve.
9. This can be stored in an airtight container for 2 to 3 days in the refrigerator.

Red Curry Pumpkin, Chickpea, and Sweet Potato Soup

Curry powder and curry paste are staples in my pantry and there is nothing I love more than using them to spice up vegetarian dishes. I also love pumpkin soup in the colder months. Put a slow cooker of this decadent soup on to keep warm, pair it with any of the bun recipes in Chapter 2, and you have an amazing vegetarian meal to serve your guests or your family.

Makes 6–8 servings | Prep Time: 20 minutes |
Total Time: 3 hours, 30 minutes to 10 hours, 30 minutes

½ cup finely diced yellow onion

2 Tbsp butter

2 tsp minced garlic

4 cups vegetable or chicken broth

1 can (29 oz/822 g) pure pumpkin

4 cups sweet potatoes, peeled and cut into ½-inch dice

1 can (19 fl oz/540 mL) chickpeas, drained and rinsed well

2½ Tbsp red curry paste

2 Tbsp soy sauce

1 Tbsp yellow curry powder

1 Tbsp brown sugar

1 tsp salt

1 can (13½ fl oz/398 mL) coconut milk

Sour cream and pepitas (pumpkin seeds), for garnish (optional)

1. In a small skillet over medium-high heat, fry the onions in the butter until soft, around 15 minutes. Add the garlic and sauté until it's browned and fragrant, then place the mixture in the slow cooker.

2. Mix in the broth, pumpkin, sweet potatoes, chickpeas, curry paste, soy sauce, curry powder, brown sugar, and salt.

3. Cook on low for 8 to 10 hours or on high for 3 to 4 hours. When ready to serve, pour in the coconut milk and mix thoroughly. Let cook until warmed again.

4. Serve topped with a swirl of sour cream and toasted pepitas if desired.

Gnocchi Pesto Caprese Salad

I whipped this up as a quick healthy lunch for Mike and me one summer day and the recipe has stuck as a favorite. Who would have thought that gnocchi are excellent served cold in a salad? This fabulously fast and delicious cheater recipe can pass for a side dish or a main meal and is perfect to take to a picnic or potluck—it's easy to make and it will get rave reviews! This recipe is a great example of how a few cheats—store-bought gnocchi and pesto—can help you eat healthier during the day.

Makes 4–5 servings as a meal, 8–10 servings as a side dish |
Prep Time: 5 minutes | Total Time: 20 minutes

1 package (17.6 oz/500 g) vacuum-packed fresh gnocchi

2 Tbsp olive oil

2 containers (7 oz/200 g) mini mini bocconcini (not a typo, they're called mini mini!)

1 container (1 lb/454 g) yellow cocktail tomatoes, halved

1 container (1 lb/454 g) red grape or cherry tomatoes

2–3 Tbsp basil pesto

Salt

¼ cup chopped fresh basil leaves

Freshly grated Romano or Parmesan cheese, for garnish

1. Prepare the gnocchi according to the package directions. Once cooked, place in a sieve and hold under cold running water until completely cooled. Transfer the gnocchi to a bowl, pour the olive oil over top, and shake or stir to coat.

2. Drain the bocconcini and add it to the bowl along with all the tomatoes and 2 tablespoons of pesto.

3. Stir to combine. Taste, and add another tablespoon of pesto if you want it stronger (I use 3). Add salt to taste, then gently mix in the fresh basil.

4. Top with freshly grated cheese.

5. Eat immediately, as the gnocchi will harden a bit if refrigerated.

Beer and Orange-Glazed Salmon

There is one word I associate with beer and orange juice: karaoke. The first and the last time I ever did karaoke. I don't usually associate cooking salmon with beer, but this cookbook is all about sharing the meals that I really and truly cook in my own house. I had salmon fillets. I had oranges in the fruit bowl, and there was beer in the fridge. (I'm Canadian, so there is always beer in the fridge or I'd have to turn over my Canuck card—yes, it's a real thing.) I hate running to the grocery store almost more than I hate gassing up my car, so beer and orange salmon it was.

Makes 4 servings | Prep Time: 5 minutes | Total Time: 15 minutes

½ cup light beer

½ cup orange juice

1 tsp garlic puree

2 tsp soy sauce

3 Tbsp liquid honey

2 Tbsp olive oil

4 salmon fillets, with or without skin

4 orange slices

Flaked sea salt, for garnish

1. In a large glass measuring cup, whisk together the beer, orange juice, garlic, soy sauce, and honey until combined. Set aside.

2. In a large skillet, heat the olive oil over medium-high heat. Place salmon skin side down in the heated oil. Sear the salmon for 2 minutes, then flip over and sear for another minute.

3. Making sure that the skillet is still searing hot, pour the beer mixture into the frying pan. The mixture should start bubbling and reducing immediately. Simmer the salmon in the beer sauce for another 4 to 5 minutes, adding in the orange slices after the first 2 minutes, continuing to cook until the sauce has reduced and the salmon is cooked to your liking.

4. Remove, top each fillet with an orange slice, and sprinkle flaked sea salt on top. Serve with rice.

◆ ◆ ◆

If you are a soy sauce junkie like I am, mix a little soy sauce with the rice you are serving the salmon on for an extra umami flavor infusion. It brings the entire dish together.

◆ ◆ ◆

Chapter Six

DAINTIES and COOKIES

✳✳✳✳✳✳✳✳✳✳

EVERYONE LOVES A GOOD DAINTY TRAY

For those who are unfamiliar with the term, "dainty" is what we on the Canadian Prairies use to describe bars, squares, and similar confections. One can't pigeonhole the term to just squares, bars, and the like, however, as my Chocolate-Dipped Banana Meringues (page 176) are also a dainty, and a tasty one at that. Perhaps the best way to describe a dainty would be "small, sweet morsels to nibble on with a cup of tea or coffee." Picture a two-tiered serving platter loaded up with small, sweet treats of assorted types and you have a dainty tray.

The dainty tray isn't always served after a meal. In fact, my Grandma Marion's dainty tray was akin to an English afternoon tea. She most definitely set up a dainty tray when company was over for an afternoon social call, and if a lot of us were visiting, she would take out her containers of frozen treats and place assorted treats on the dainty tray to thaw out ahead of time. When she was alone, or just had one or two of us grandkids with her, she had her own routine. In the middle of the afternoon, she would have her cup of tea with one or two of her favorite small treats on a plate. I think it was a treasured time for her to relax and refuel during her busy days on the farm, where she was always going from early light to dark. I can still picture her in her little eating nook in her farmhouse kitchen with a cup of steaming hot tea and a dainty or two.

When you create a dainty tray, remember to slice everything into small tidbits—the point is to be able to try more than just one treat from the tray in small amounts, and tea time is about tasting, not filling up. The point is to have one or two (or three if your mom didn't catch you) dainties while chatting. So, when hosting, your dainty tray should have a variety of four or five types. Slice your standard-serving-size bars in half, so guests can taste a few with less guilt!

You can make these treats ahead of time and freeze them as my grandmother did; just make sure to cut the squares beforehand and store the baked goods well divided, with waxed paper between them, in airtight containers, and you'll have your own arsenal of entertaining treats at the ready. All the treats in this section are freezer-friendly, except for the puffed wheat squares, which I find lose their chewy goodness once frozen.

My grandma's treats ranged from cookies to bars, with bars being her favorite thing to bake.

I too love baking bars, and I have included some delicious bar recipes in this section, my favorite being my new Piña Colada Sour Cream Squares (page 180). Whoa, Nellie! Now those are good! I've also included classics like butter tarts and one of my favorite lemon bars recipes, because I think that no dainty tray can be considered complete without them.

Happy baking everyone!

Piña Colada Sour Cream Squares (page 180)

Classic Canadian Butter Tarts

I was scolded for leaving butter tarts out of my first book. Heavily. Thus proving that there is no doubt that we Canadians love our butter tarts. With this recipe, you can use premade tart shells or whip up a classic butter pastry; it's the filling that is the star. While most butter tart fillings use basically the same ingredients, my version uses heavy cream and salted butter to make this filling the richest yet. Another delicious little Canadian secret is the maple syrup instead of corn syrup, to add the perfect flavor to traditional butter tarts. These can be made into mini tarts if you are looking for smaller treats: simply make them in mini muffin pans and use a 2-inch biscuit cutter.

Makes 1 dozen tarts | Prep Time: 20 minutes |
Total Time: 1 hour, 40 minutes, including chilling

Classic Butter Pastry

2½ cups all-purpose flour, plus extra
for your work surface

2 tsp white sugar

1 tsp salt

1 cup unsalted butter, frozen

¼–½ cup ice water

Butter Tart Filling

1 cup packed brown sugar

⅔ cup Thompson seedless raisins or
currants

1 egg, beaten

⅓ cup melted salted butter

2–4 Tbsp maple syrup or corn syrup

2 Tbsp heavy cream or milk

1 tsp vanilla extract

1 tsp lemon juice or vinegar
(optional; see Tips)

1. To make the pastry, place the flour, sugar, and salt in a large mixing bowl and whisk together. Using a cheese grater, grate the frozen butter into the flour mixture. Mix in the butter with a pastry cutter or 2 knives until the flour mixture is crumbly, and the butter is the size of peas. Add the ice water, 1 table-spoon at a time, tossing the flour with a fork to mix, just until the dough comes together when pinched between your fingers. Form the dough into a ball. Divide into 2 and form 2 disks. Wrap each disk securely in plastic wrap and refrigerate for 1 hour. You can also store the dough overnight.

2. When ready to bake, preheat the oven to 375°F. Have a 12-cup muffin tin on hand.

3. Sprinkle your work surface with flour. Remove one disk from the fridge and let it sit on the work surface for a few minutes. Roll out the dough until it's ⅛-inch thick. Cut out six 4-inch circles, placing each circle in a well in the muffin tin to form a tart, making sure that the dough edges stand out above the muffin tin slightly. Repeat with the second dough disk.

4. To make the filling, in a large bowl, mix together all the filling ingredients until well combined. Fill each tart shell three-quarters of the way full of the filling mixture. There should be exactly enough filling.

5. Bake for 17 to 20 minutes, or until the filling is bubbling and the pastry has browned.

Butter Tart Tips

➤ You can add 1 teaspoon of vinegar or lemon juice to the filling to cut the sweetness.

➤ Corn syrup offers a more traditional taste, but I prefer maple syrup for a gooier tart.

➤ Using heavy cream instead of the usual milk makes for a richer tart. Try it and see!

➤ Currants are the fruit of choice for purists, but I love raisins the best. You can also add pecans, walnuts, or if you really want to be sacrilegious, try some shredded coconut or chocolate chips!

Black-Bottomed Butter Tart Squares

Try to say that title 5 times in a row! I decided that the traditional butter tart square needed a chocolate revamp—and it's one of those ideas that *really* worked out well. Again, if you are taking this to a party or function, you will absolutely be asked for the recipe from anyone who is familiar with the normal butter tart square recipe. Just tell them to buy this cookbook—for them and a few (or 10) family members.

Makes 25 squares | Prep Time: 15 minutes | Total Time: 35 minutes

CHOCOLATE CRUST

1 cup chocolate cookie crumbs

¼ cup all-purpose flour

6 Tbsp melted salted butter

BUTTER TART TOPPING

2 large eggs

1 cup packed brown sugar

1 Tbsp cornstarch

2 Tbsp heavy cream

2 tsp vanilla extract

¼ cup melted salted butter

Pinch of salt

2 cups Thompson seedless raisins

1. Preheat the oven to 350°F.
2. To make the crust, place the crust ingredients in a bowl and mix until the melted butter is completely incorporated.
3. Press the mixture into an ungreased 8- × 8-inch or 9- × 9-inch baking pan and bake for 15 minutes. Remove and set aside to cool slightly. Leave the oven switched on.
4. To make the topping, in a medium bowl or a large measuring cup, mix the eggs and brown sugar together until creamy. Add the cornstarch, cream, vanilla, butter, and salt. Mix until smooth.
5. Stir in the raisins and then pour the mixture onto the chocolate crust. Return the pan to the oven and bake until the topping is beautifully browned, 18 to 20 minutes. Remove and cool in the pan completely before cutting into squares.
6. These can be stored in an airtight container for 2 to 3 days in the refrigerator, or frozen in a freezer-safe container for up to 3 months.

Chocolate-Dipped Banana Meringues

Here's that fake banana flavor I love so much! Meringues are a delicious gluten-free dessert favorite, and these ones are especially jazzed up. Not only are they banana flavored, but they're dipped in chocolate too. Make meringues on non-humid days, as humidity can wreak havoc on them.

Makes 24 meringues (depending on their shape and size) | Prep Time: 30 minutes | Total Time: 2 hours, 30 minutes to 3 hours, 30 minutes

Meringues

5 egg whites, room temperature

1½ cups white sugar

½ tsp white vinegar

4 tsp banana flavoring

yellow food coloring

Chocolate Dip

1 cup semi-sweet chocolate chips

2 tsp butter

◆ ◆ ◆

You can freeze meringues in an airtight container for up to a month, but they will break if tossed around. Make sure they aren't exposed to any moisture or humidity.

◆ ◆ ◆

1. Preheat the oven to 200°F. Line 2 baking sheets with parchment paper and set aside.
2. To make the meringues, using a handheld or stand mixer, beat the egg whites on the highest speed until stiff peaks form, around 5 minutes. Stop the mixer, add the sugar and vinegar, then mix until thick and shiny. Stir in the banana flavoring and yellow food coloring, a few drops at a time, until the preferred depth of color is achieved, then beat until the color is mixed through.
3. Spoon the egg white mixture into a pastry bag fitted with your desired tip. (I prefer a large star tip.) Pipe the mixture onto baking sheets in the desired size. Try to make them the same size so they all dry out at around the same time.
4. Bake for 1 to 2 hours, or until crisp and dried out. Start to check the meringues after 1 hour. When they are ready, you shouldn't see any beads of moisture on them and they should sound hollow when lightly tapped. Check every 15 minutes after the 1-hour point. Do not let them brown. Once they are dried out, turn the oven off without opening the door and leave the meringues in there for an additional hour. Remove and cool completely on the baking sheets.
5. To make the dip, melt the chocolate chips with the butter in a microwave-safe dish in your microwave, stirring every 20 seconds until melted and smooth.
6. Line 2 baking sheets with waxed paper. Dip the tops of the fully cooled meringues into the chocolate, then place on the cookie sheets to harden.
7. Keep stored in an airtight container at room temperature for up to 3 days.

Saskatoon Cheesecake Brownies

Here's a recipe to use up your summertime bounty of saskatoon berries (or blueberries) in a decadent cheesecake brownie. Saskatoon berries aren't often paired with chocolate, but trust me, it's a delicious combination!

Makes 30 brownies | Prep Time: 30 minutes |
Total Time: Approximately 1 hour, 20 minutes, plus setting

SASKATOON SAUCE

2 cups fresh or frozen saskatoon berries

1 cup cold water

½ cup white sugar

3 Tbsp cornstarch

1 Tbsp lemon juice

BROWNIE BATTER

1½ cups salted butter

3 cups white sugar

1½ cups Dutch process cocoa powder

6 eggs, beaten

1½ cups all-purpose flour

CREAM CHEESE TOPPING

2 packages (8 oz/226 g each) cream cheese, softened and cubed

½ cup white sugar

1 egg

½ tsp vanilla extract

1. To make the sauce, in a medium-sized saucepan place the berries, ¾ cup of the water, and the sugar. Bring to a slow boil over medium-high heat and cook for 10 minutes, stirring occasionally, until the berries have softened. Whisk the cornstarch into the remaining ¼ cup of water and then rapidly whisk into the berry mixture. Stir in the lemon juice. Cook until the sauce thickens, then remove from the heat. You want the filling to resemble thick pie filling. If needed, add more cornstarch to achieve this. Set aside to cool.

2. Preheat the oven to 350°F. Grease a 9- × 13-inch baking dish and set aside.

3. To make the brownies, melt the butter in a medium saucepan over low heat. Remove from the heat and stir in the sugar until mixed in thoroughly, then add the cocoa, stirring until completely smooth.

4. Add the eggs and stir to combine thoroughly.

5. Add the flour and stir it in until just combined—do not overmix. Pour into the prepared pan.

6. To make the topping, in a stand mixer fitted with the paddle attachment, place the cream cheese, sugar, egg, and vanilla. Beat until smooth. Drop by the spoonful on top of the brownie mixture, followed by the cooled saskatoon sauce.

7. Take a butter knife and swirl the cream cheese and sauce together, creating a marbled look.

8. Bake for 45 to 50 minutes, until the topping starts to brown at the edges. The center will still be a bit wobbly. Remove and cool in the pan until set, about 4 to 5 hours.

9. These can be stored in an airtight container for 2 to 3 days in the refrigerator, or frozen in a freezer-safe container for up to 3 months.

Piña Colada Sour Cream Squares

"Don't tell Kari you sent these home with me. I'm literally going to drive around the corner, park the car, and eat them before I get there."

And that, my friends, is how good these squares are. (Some of them did make it home to his wife Kari, by the way.) These crumbly coconut pineapple squares taste like one big Piña Colada cocktail was baked into a square.

Makes 25 squares | Prep Time: 20 minutes | Total Time: 1 hour to 1 hour, 10 minutes

Oatmeal Crumble Crust

½ cup butter

½ cup packed brown sugar

1 cup all-purpose flour

1 cup rolled oats (also known as old-fashioned oats)

½ cup unsweetened shredded coconut

Pineapple Sour Cream Filling

1 egg

¾ cup sour cream

½ cup white sugar

1 Tbsp cornstarch

¼ tsp salt

1 can (14 fl oz/398 mL) pineapple rings, drained and cut into large chunks

1. Preheat the oven to 350°F. Spray an 8- × 8-inch baking pan lightly with cooking spray.
2. To make the crust, in a stand mixer fitted with the paddle attachment, cream together the butter and sugar until combined. Add the flour, beating constantly until smooth. Add the oats and coconut and mix until everything is incorporated completely.
3. Press half of the mixture firmly into the prepared baking pan, reserving the other half. Bake for 6 minutes, then remove and set the pan on a wire rack.
4. To make the filling, in a heavy saucepan, place the egg, sour cream, sugar, cornstarch, and salt. Whisk until smooth and creamy. Heat on medium-high heat for 8 to 10 minutes, stirring constantly, until thick and creamy, like a pudding. Remove from the heat and stir in the pineapple chunks.
5. Pour this mixture onto the still-warm baked crust, spreading it out in an even layer. Scatter the reserved crust mixture evenly over the filling.
6. Bake for 30 to 35 minutes or until the top is well browned and the filling is set—the bars shouldn't wobble when you shake the pan slightly.
7. Remove and cool completely in the pan before slicing into squares.
8. These can be stored in an airtight container for 2 to 3 days in the refrigerator, or frozen in a freezer-safe container for up to 3 months.

Classic Puffed Wheat Squares

I'm going to tell you right now that the problem with puffed wheat squares is that if you overcook that dang sauce you will be breaking your teeth on the squares when they are done, and your dentist might be laughing all the way to the bank. To give them the perfect firmness, I've started using marshmallows and barely cooking the corn syrup. I can't stress this enough: if you boil it too long, you've basically made hard candy. But if done correctly, these squares are the BEST cereal bars ever!

Makes 2 dozen squares | Prep Time: 10 minutes | Total Time: 40 minutes

10 cups puffed wheat

½ cup salted butter

½ cup light corn syrup

1 cup white sugar

¼ cup packed brown sugar

6 Tbsp Dutch process cocoa powder

1–2 cups mini marshmallows (1 cup = chewy, 2 cups = even chewier)

1 tsp vanilla extract

1. Line a 9- × 13-inch baking tray with parchment paper.
2. Place the puffed wheat in a very large bowl. I use my large Tupperware bowl that every Canadian grandma has owned as a dough bowl at one time. You know the one!
3. Place the butter, corn syrup, both sugars, and cocoa powder in a medium saucepan. Bring to a boil over medium-high heat, stirring occasionally. Let boil for 1 minute, not stirring, then remove from heat and stir in the marshmallows all at once, followed by the vanilla, until the marshmallows are melted in completely.
4. Pour the mixture over the puffed wheat and mix well.
5. Press firmly into the prepared baking tray.
6. Let sit for at least 30 minutes at room temperature, then cut into squares. Do not refrigerate or they will turn to stone.
7. Some people swear they have frozen these with success; however, all that proves is that they have a better dental plan than I do. Keep them in an airtight container at room temperature for 2 to 3 days.

Lemon Cheesecake Squares

Give me all of the lemon, all of the time. Sometimes after a heavy meal you are looking for something lighter, and lemon desserts can fool us into believing that they are indeed lighter in some way. They usually aren't, but there is just something about lemon and cheesecake together that makes you feel like you are indeed having a sweet light bite.

Makes 25 squares | Prep Time: 10 minutes |
Total Time: 50 minutes to 1 hour, plus chilling

Shortbread Crust

1 cup all-purpose flour

¼ cup cornstarch

¼ cup white sugar

½ cup salted butter

2 Tbsp grated lemon zest

Cream Cheese Layer

1 package (8 oz/226 g) cream cheese, cubed

½ cup white sugar

1 egg

Lemon Layer

4 extra-large eggs, room temperature

1⅔ cups white sugar

⅔ cup all-purpose flour

⅔ cup lemon juice (2 to 3 large lemons)

Icing sugar for sprinkling (optional)

1. Preheat the oven to 350°F. Grease a 9- × 9-inch baking pan. Cut out a 9- × 9-inch square of parchment paper and lay on top of the greased bottom of the pan.

2. For the crust, use a pastry blender to combine the flour, cornstarch, sugar, butter, and lemon zest until the mixture is coarse crumbs, with the butter worked in. Press the dough into the greased baking pan, on top of the parchment paper. Bake for 15 minutes, until lightly browned. Remove and place the pan on a wire rack to cool slightly. Leave the oven switched on.

3. For the cream cheese layer, fit a stand mixer fitted with the paddle attachment. Beat the cream cheese and sugar together until light and creamy, 3 to 4 minutes. Beat in the egg completely, then pour the mixture onto the warm crust. Return to the oven and bake for 10 to 15 minutes, until slightly set on top. You need to have the top cooked in a slight crust so the lemon layer doesn't seep through when poured on top. Remove. Leave the oven switched on.

4. For the lemon layer, whisk together all the ingredients by hand. Gently pour over the cream cheese layer, trying not to disturb it. Spread out the lemon in an even layer.

5. Return to the hot oven and bake for another 25 to 30 minutes, until the filling is just set in the center.

6. Cool at room temperature, then refrigerate uncovered to let the filling set completely. This should be refrigerated at least 3 hours, but more time may be needed.

7. Sprinkle with icing sugar if desired. Slice into squares to serve.

9. These can be stored in an airtight container for 2 to 3 days in the refrigerator, or frozen in a freezer-safe container for up to 3 months.

Dirty Chocolate Chip Cookies

I know that your mind went straight to the gutter (because mine did) but dirty cookies are simply cookies that you roll in crumbs of another cookie or baking crumbs. Basically, you make them dirty with some other tasty thing! The something else in this recipe was one of my favorite store-bought cookies, the chocolate ones with the vanilla center. The name of those cookies rhymes with "sm'oreos."

You can roll them in chocolate baking crumbs, graham cracker crumbs, broken up chocolate bars . . . basically the sky's the limit when it comes to dirty cookies!

Makes 2–3 dozen cookies | Prep Time: 15 minutes | Total Time: 25 to 30 minutes

12–16 Oreos or another cream-filled chocolate cookie, broken into small crumbs and tiny chunks

½ cup butter

½ cup white sugar

1 cup packed brown sugar

2 eggs

2 tsp vanilla extract

2¼ cups all-purpose flour

1 tsp baking soda

1 tsp salt

2 cups semi-sweet chocolate chips

1. Preheat the oven to 350°F. Line 2 baking sheets with parchment paper. Place the cookie crumbs in a shallow bowl.

2. Place the butter, white sugar, and brown sugar in a stand mixer fitted with the paddle attachment and beat until fluffy, 3 to 4 minutes. Add the eggs, one at a time, beating until combined. Add the vanilla and beat until mixed in.

3. In a bowl, whisk together the flour, baking soda, and salt; gradually add to the butter mixture, beating on low speed until well blended. Stir in the chocolate chips until combined.

4. Take a ball of dough roughly half the size of a golf ball and roll it in the broken cookies, making sure you press hard enough to get the cookie crumbs embedded well into the dough.

5. Place on the prepared baking sheets.

6. Bake for 10 to 12 minutes, or until the edges are lightly browned. Cool on the baking sheets for 5 minutes, then transfer to wire racks.

7. Keep in a sealed container for up to 3 days or in the freezer for up to 3 months. You can also freeze the dough in a freezer-safe bag for up to 3 months.

Pistachio Pudding Cookies

cheater!

These are my favorite cookies, of course! I decided one day that I needed to make pudding cookies with my all-time favorite pudding mix flavor—pistachio. Even though it's an easy cheater recipe, this is the one cookie recipe that people are excited to see me bring to potlucks or picnics. So, have the recipe handy when you take these to a party, because it's a forgone conclusion that you will be asked for it!

Makes 2–3 dozen cookies | Prep Time: 10 minutes | Total Time: 20 to 25 minutes

1 cup salted butter, softened

1 cup white sugar

1 package (3.4 oz/99 g) pistachio instant pudding

2 eggs

2 cups all-purpose flour

1 tsp baking soda

1 cup white chocolate chips

½ cup crushed pistachios

1. Preheat the oven to 350°F. Line a baking sheet with parchment paper.
2. In a stand mixer fitted with the paddle attachment, beat the butter, sugar, and pudding mix together until creamy.
3. Add the eggs, one at a time, beating well after each addition.
4. Whisk the flour and baking soda together in a separate bowl, and then slowly add it to the butter mixture, mixing on low speed the entire time.
5. Once it's all mixed completely, fold in the chocolate chips.
6. Using a tablespoon-sized cookie scoop, create a cookie ball, roll the top of the dough ball in the crushed pistachios, then place the dough balls onto the prepared baking sheet, about 1 inch apart.
7. Bake for 9 to 12 minutes, until the bottoms of the cookies are slightly browned.
8. Let cool on baking sheet for at least 5 minutes before transferring to wire racks to cool completely.

How to Make Cake Mix Cookies

cheater!

Anyone over the age of 10 can make these, including spouses who profess they can't bake. You are going to give your spouse this recipe and grab a glass of wine: it's time for a couples' baking session at 9 p.m., where you drink wine and watch them bake the cookies. Romantic, right?

The only cake mixes that I wouldn't use in this recipe are angel food cake ones, but other than that the sky's the limit. Lemon, carrot cake, cherry chip, rainbow, you name it— you can make cookies from it!

Makes 2 dozen cookies | Prep Time: 12 minutes | Total Time: 35 minutes

1 box (15¼ oz/432 g) cake mix

½ cup butter, softened

2 eggs, beaten

1. Preheat the oven to 350°F. Line 2 baking sheets with parchment paper.
2. Place the ingredients in a medium mixing bowl and mix together using a hand mixer or stand mixer.
3. Using a tablespoon-sized cookie scoop, drop dough portions onto the baking sheet about 2 inches apart.
4. Cool in the refrigerator (or outside at any time of the year, if you live in Alberta) for 10 minutes.
5. Bake for 12 to 15 minutes, until the edges are firm and baked, and the middle is set.
6. Remove and cool on baking sheets completely.
7. These can be stored in an airtight container for 2 to 3 days at room temperature or frozen in a freezer-safe container for up to 3 months.

✦ ✦ ✦

Life Moments You Need This Recipe for:

1. *"I signed you up for cookies at the class party tomorrow, Mommy! What kind did you make?"*
➤ *If they aren't old enough, this recipe is easier than your going to the store. I promise.*

2. *"Oh, hey, hon, I put you down for cookies for the office potluck tomorrow . . . and forgot to tell you."*
➤ *If they are old enough, get them up at 6 a.m. to make these cookies themselves.*

✦ ✦ ✦

Chocolate Coconut Chews

These cookies happened by accident. I threw a bunch of ingredients together in my stand mixer bowl one weekend, hoping that they would magically turn into a cookie—and they did. These are like a thin, chewy brownie and are probably the best cookie that I have ever dipped into a glass of milk.

Makes 3 dozen cookies | Prep Time: 10 minutes | Total Time: 20 minutes

1 can (13.4 oz/380 g) dulce de leche caramel-flavored sauce

¼ cup salted butter, softened

1 tsp vanilla extract

1 cup chocolate cookie crumbs

½ cup all-purpose flour

¼ cup Dutch process cocoa powder

1 tsp baking powder

1 cup unsweetened shredded coconut

1 cup semi-sweet chocolate chips

1. Preheat the oven to 375°F. Line 2 baking sheets with parchment paper.
2. In a stand mixer fitted with the paddle attachment, beat the dulce de leche with the butter until smooth, 2 to 3 minutes. Add the vanilla and beat well. Add the cookie crumbs and mix on low speed until combined.
3. In a medium-sized bowl, whisk together the flour, cocoa, and baking powder. With the mixer on low, slowly add the chocolate crumb mixture, beating the ingredients in well.
4. Stop the mixer and add the coconut. Resume mixing at the lowest speed until the coconut is just incorporated. Stir in the chocolate chips by hand.
5. Drop by tablespoonful onto the prepared baking sheets, 2 inches apart.
6. Bake for 8 to 10 minutes, until the edges are crispy and set. The centers can be a little underbaked.
7. Remove and cool completely on the baking sheets—they will stick to a wire rack!
8. These can be stored in an airtight container for 2 to 3 days at room temperature or frozen in a freezer-safe container for up to 3 months.

Spicy Molasses Oatmeal Raisin Cookies

These cookies combine my two favorite cookies, spicy gingersnaps and oatmeal raisin cookies—and they've been a staple in my house ever since I perfected them. If you are a molasses lover, you can use cooking molasses for a deeper, bolder flavor in these cookies.

Makes 3–4 dozen cookies | Prep Time: 10 minutes | Total Time: 20 minutes

¾ cup butter

¾ cup white sugar

⅓ cup packed brown sugar

1 egg

¼ cup fancy molasses

1¼ cups all-purpose flour

1 tsp baking soda

1 tsp ground cinnamon

½ tsp ground cloves

½ tsp ground ginger

½ tsp salt

2 cups rolled oats

1 cup seedless Thompson raisins

1. Preheat the oven to 350°F. Line 2 baking sheets with parchment paper.
2. In a stand mixer fitted with the paddle attachment, beat the butter and both sugars together until smooth, about 2 to 3 minutes. Add the egg and beat well, and then add the molasses, beating until combined.
3. In a medium bowl, whisk together the flour, baking soda, cinnamon, cloves, ginger, and salt. With the mixer on low speed, beat the flour mixture into the butter mixture until thoroughly combined.
4. Stir in the rolled oats and the raisins by hand until they are fully incorporated.
5. Drop by the heaping tablespoonful onto the prepared baking sheets, 2 inches apart.
6. Bake for 8 to 10 minutes, until the edges are fully cooked and set and the tops are browned.
7. Remove and let cool on the sheets completely.
8. These can be stored in an airtight container for 2 to 3 days at room temperature or frozen in a freezer-safe container for up to 3 months.

Bakery-Style Thick and Chewy Peanut Butter Cookies

This recipe is going to get you the thickest, chewiest, closest-to-a-bakery-style peanut butter cookie you've ever had. The secret is to underbake them slightly (always do this for a chewy cookie) and then flatten them slightly when they come out of the oven. If it's humid where you live, or it's rainy, simply add another 2 to 3 tablespoons of flour to the mix to combat the extra moisture. When you want to bake super-thick cookies, you have to watch the dough moisture more than with other cookies. These are large and in charge cookies!

Makes 12–16 cookies | Prep Time: 15 minutes | Total Time: 30 minutes

½ cup butter, softened

1 cup packed brown sugar

1 large egg

½ cup peanut butter (creamy or crunchy, up to you)

2 tsp vanilla extract

1¼ cups all-purpose flour

½ tsp baking soda

½ tsp salt

2 cups semi-sweet chocolate chips (optional)

1. Preheat the oven to 375°F. Line 2 baking sheets with parchment paper.
2. In a stand mixer fitted with the paddle attachment, cream the butter and sugar together until light and fluffy.
3. Beat in the egg until combined, then add in the peanut butter and vanilla. Mix well.
4. Whisk the flour, baking soda, and salt together. Add to the butter mixture and mix together thoroughly.
5. Mix in the chocolate chips (if using) by hand, until evenly distributed throughout the dough.
6. Using a standard ice cream scoop, fill the scoop with dough, scraping the dough level with the straight edge of the scoop.
7. Place the dough by rounded scoop onto the prepared baking sheets, about 2 inches apart.
8. Bake for 14 to 15 minutes, or until golden brown all over.
9. Remove from the oven. The cookies should still be in a dome shape. Using a flat spatula or egg flipper, press each cookie down slightly. They should be about ½ inch to ¾ inch thick.
10. Leave the cookies on the baking sheets to cool completely after flattening.
11. These can be stored in an airtight container for 2 to 3 days at room temperature or frozen in a freezer-safe container for up to 3 months.

Chapter Seven

PORTABLE DESSERTS

✽✽✽✽✽✽✽✽✽✽✽✽✽

PORTABLE DESSERTS

I love a delicious dessert that travels with you. Could there be anything better than a dessert on the go? I honestly don't think so.

It will come as no surprise that even before I wrote my first cookbook (which comprises 100 percent dessert recipes) I was known as the person to ask to bring desserts to a gathering. I would bake cookies and take them to work with me for my shift mates and send all sorts of goodies with Mike to work to get rid of them. I once brought cake in the trunk of my car to send home with friends after a night out on the town. When you bake as many desserts as it takes to build up a substantial recipe index on a website, it becomes a challenge to give them away, much less eat them. Luckily, we both had workplaces with staff kitchens where we could dump the goodies and run before anyone yelled at us for being diet wreckers. Then we started working from home and had nowhere to get rid of all the sweet treats. Who knew that there was a bonus to going into an office every day?

I love desserts in pans, in containers, in trifle dishes, and especially cakes in cake carriers. Oh, those are my very favorite as I get to use some of my vintage cake carriers and say to Mike "See? I told you that I needed this cake carrier!"

All the recipes in this chapter are easy to take with you to a party. Everything that is made in the pan can even stay in its pan in the fridge or freezer, until you are ready to serve it. Just make sure that your hostess has room for a pan in her fridge! Simply keep the pans wrapped up in two layers of plastic wrap, followed by a layer of aluminum foil, and they will be ready to go when you are. Easy as pie!

One cake in particular that you shouldn't miss is the Australian Lumberjack Cake (page 207). An old friend from high school lived down under for many years and brought this cake to my attention. If you love dates and apples, make this cake now. I also suggest it as a top choice for taking to potlucks and parties, as I can almost guarantee that no one will have tried it before. Have the recipe handy, for sure, because the date lovers in the crowd will insist that you share it.

I am also extremely proud of the Creamy Baked Rice Pudding recipe on page 200. Rice pudding is one of the most beloved Prairie desserts, yet it can be hit-or-miss for home cooks since sugars can interfere with the cooking process of the rice. Never fear, I have come up with a surefire way to make rice pudding perfectly every time.

Baked in a pan, stored in a pan, served from a pan, or even eaten from a pan (I won't judge), the desserts on the following pages are a gathering of the best simple yet delicious crowd-pleasing desserts for the busy baker on the go.

Creamy Baked Rice Pudding (page 200)

Creamy Baked Rice Pudding

Rice pudding is THE Canadian Prairie comfort dessert! But it can be hit or miss when it comes to cooking the rice completely as the sugar can interfere with the cooking process, the same way as it can with baked beans (and that's why baked beans take *allll* day!). So I was determined to come up with a new Prairie rice pudding recipe that works every time and is still the creamiest, most decadently easy rice pudding around—and I think that I've done it! The trick is to add the sugar found in the condensed milk AFTER the rice cooks, to ensure 100 percent success.

Makes 12 servings | Prep Time: 10 minutes | Total Time: 2 hours, 40 minutes

4 cups whole milk

½ cup water

1 cup medium- or short-grain white rice

1 tsp vanilla extract

1 tsp ground cinnamon (optional; I like only nutmeg in mine)

½ tsp salt

½ tsp ground nutmeg

1 cup Thompson raisins

1 can (13.4 oz/380 g) sweetened condensed milk

1. Preheat the oven to 325°F. Grease a 2¼-quart lidded casserole dish.

2. Pour the milk and water into the casserole dish. Stir in the rice, vanilla, cinnamon, salt, and nutmeg. Put the lid on the casserole dish.

3. Bake for 1 hour, then stir everything thoroughly.

4. Continue baking, still with the lid on, for another hour. Check to make sure that the rice is cooked to your liking, then add the raisins and condensed milk, stirring until mixed in completely.

5. Return to the oven and bake uncovered for another 30 minutes.

6. Serve while hot.

7. To store, covered the casserole dish with 2 layers of plastic wrap, followed by aluminum foil, and store in the refrigerator for 2 to 3 days or freeze for up to 3 months.

Chocolate Satin Glaze

An excellent chocolate satin glaze will take you everywhere in the land of baking. From scones to cupcakes, doughnuts to cakes, a chocolate satin glaze is often the finishing touch that elevates a baked good from great to spectacular.

Makes 1½ cups | Prep Time: 5 minutes | Total Time: 25 minutes, including setting

¾ cup semi-sweet chocolate chips

2 Tbsp salted butter

2 Tbsp light corn syrup

½ tsp vanilla extract

1. Place the chocolate chips, butter, and corn syrup in a large microwave-safe measuring cup.
2. Microwave for 45 seconds, stirring every 15 seconds, until the mixture is smooth.
3. Stir in the vanilla.
4. Pour the warm glaze over the chosen baked good and let drizzle down the sides. Let the glaze set for 20 to 25 minutes before slicing.

Black Magic Mystery Cake

Doesn't the title of this cake sound so deliciously evil? So very delightfully wicked? Well, folks, the reason it's called "mystery cake" is that it has tomato soup in it. Oh yes, I have heard from a lot of readers, and tomato soup cake is THE cake of the Prairies. A local Edmonton food writer friend—who shall remain unnamed unless she chooses to come forward, but her initials are L.F.—told me this was *the* cake from her childhood. This is my dark, delicious (dare I say mysterious?) chocolate version of the more common spiced cake.

Makes 15 servings | Prep Time: 15 minutes | Total Time: 1 hour to 1 hour, 5 minutes

½ cup butter

1 cup white sugar

1 cup packed brown sugar

½ cup vegetable oil

4 eggs

2 cups all-purpose flour

¾ cup Dutch process cocoa powder

¼ cup cornstarch

2 tsp baking powder

1 tsp salt

1 can (10 oz/284 mL) condensed tomato soup

¾ cup heavy cream

1 Tbsp vanilla extract

1 batch Chocolate Satin Glaze (page 201)

1. Preheat the oven to 350°F. Grease and flour a 9- × 13-inch glass or ceramic dish and set aside.

2. In a stand mixer fitted with the paddle attachment, place the butter and both sugars. Beat until they are combined, about 1 minute, then pour in the oil. Beat until light and fluffy, around 2 to 3 minutes. Beat in the eggs, one at a time, until fully incorporated.

3. In a medium-sized bowl, whisk together the flour, cocoa, cornstarch, baking powder, and salt. In a large measuring glass, whisk together the tomato soup, cream, and vanilla.

4. Pour half of the dry ingredients into the butter mixture. Beat until completely mixed in. Pour half of the tomato soup mixture into the butter mixture and beat in completely. Repeat with the remaining dry ingredients, and end with the tomato mixture. Beat for another 1 to 2 minutes on medium speed, until the mixture is smooth.

5. Pour the batter into the prepared dish. Bake for 35 to 40 minutes, or until a cake tester or toothpick inserted into the center of the cake comes out clean. Remove and start to cool, in the dish, on a wire rack.

6. Prepare the Chocolate Satin Glaze and spread over the still-warm cake. Let cool at room temperature, uncovered.

7. To store, cover the cake pan with 2 layers of plastic wrap, followed by aluminum foil, and store in the refrigerator for 2 to 3 days or freeze for up to 3 months.

Chocolate Apricot Wafer Slice

I have never understood the lack of apricot dessert love here in Canada. When I went to Paris for the first time, many years ago, I was thrilled with how every bakery had 2 or 3 apricot pastries or desserts. All the pastries I ate (all in the name of research, of course!) used apricots from a can, which are readily available year-round.

If you're from Manitoba, you might be familiar with this dessert, but it was a complete novelty for everyone in Saskatchewan whom I served it to.

I stumbled on this recipe while I was going through my Grandma Kay's recipes and was thrilled to see it had apricots! This is one of my favorite new desserts. If you are so inclined, try peaches in this as well.

Makes 10–12 servings | Prep Time: 30 minutes | Total Time: 6 hours, 30 minutes

Chocolate Crust

1½ packages (36 wafers) rectangular icing-filled chocolate wafers, crushed fine, with extra for topping

½ cup melted salted butter

Icing Layer

2 cups icing sugar

½ cup salted butter, softened

3 Tbsp heavy cream

1 tsp vanilla extract

2 cans (14 fl oz/398 mL) apricot halves in light syrup, or 30–35 home canned apricots, drained

Whipped Topping

2 cups whipping cream

2 tsp granulated sugar

1 tsp vanilla extract

1. To make the crust, mix together the wafer crumbs and butter to thoroughly combine, then press into a 9- × 13-inch baking pan. Chill while preparing the next components.
2. To make the icing layer, in a stand mixer fitted with the paddle attachment, place the icing sugar, butter, cream, and vanilla. Beat, starting on low and increasing the speed to high, until smooth and creamy, 3 to 4 minutes. Spread over the crust in an even layer.
3. Take the drained apricots and place them on top of the icing layer, flat side down in one layer. Reserve a few apricots for the topping.
4. To make the topping, in a large bowl, use a handheld mixer to beat the whipping cream, sugar, and vanilla together until the cream is light and fluffy and forms peaks when you lift the beaters. Spread over the apricots. Sprinkle the top with crushed chocolate wafers and a few apricots for garnish.
5. Cover and refrigerate for 6 hours or overnight. Slice and serve straight from the pan. This will store in the pan, covered, in the fridge for 2 to 3 days but does not freeze well.

Australian Lumberjack Cake

Sometimes, no matter how loudly you shout out to the world that a recipe is amazing, you get crickets. This is one of those recipes, and that was why I had to include it in this cookbook. This cake is—no word of a lie—our very favorite cake now. The apples and dates help it bake up into the most decadently moist cake I've ever eaten. This recipe is thanks to a high school friend who lived in Australia for many years and loved this cake. On her return she described the ingredients and asked me to come up with a recipe—I hope it does the original cake justice!

15–20 servings | Prep Time: 30 minutes | Total Time: 1 hour, 40 minutes

CAKE

1½ cups peeled, diced crisp apple (Honeycrisp, Ambrosia, Fuji)

1½ cups diced dates

1½ tsp baking soda

1½ cups boiling water

¾ cup butter

1½ cups white sugar

1 egg

1½ tsp vanilla extract

2¼ cups all-purpose flour

¾ tsp salt

BROILED COCONUT TOPPING

1½ cups sweetened shredded coconut

¾ cup packed brown sugar

6 Tbsp salted butter

⅓ cup milk

1. Preheat the oven to 350°F. Grease a 9- × 13-inch baking dish and set aside.
2. To make the cake, place the apples, dates, and baking soda in a medium-sized bowl and mix to combine. Pour the boiling water over top. Allow to cool to lukewarm.
3. In a stand mixer fitted with the paddle attachment, cream the butter with the sugar until light and fluffy.
4. Add the egg and vanilla and beat well.
5. In a small bowl, whisk together the flour and salt. Starting with the flour and alternating with the apple mixture, beat the two mixtures into the butter mixture until both are combined completely.
6. Pour the batter into the prepared dish and bake for about 1 hour, or until a cake tester inserted in the center comes out clean. Remove and place on top of the stove or on a wire rack. Leave the oven switched on.
7. To make the topping, place the coconut, brown sugar, butter, and milk in a microwave-safe dish and heat in 20-second increments until the butter is melted. (Or place the ingredients in a small saucepan and melt the butter on the stove top over low heat.) Stir the ingredients together to blend completely.
8. Spread over the hot cake and return the cake to the oven for another 10 minutes, or until the topping is golden brown.
9. Serve warm or cold.
10. To store, cover the pan with 2 layers of plastic wrap, followed by aluminum foil, and store in the refrigerator for 2 to 3 days or freeze for up to 3 months.

Streusel Apple Pie Bread Pudding

This recipe doubles as a dessert and a decadent breakfast—the choice is up to you! (I'd choose both, of course.) It does have to be prepped the night before, though, to make sure that the bread soaks up all the delicious milk mixture. It's so simple—take it out the next day and bake it up!

Makes 10–12 servings | Prep Time: 30 minutes |
Total Time: 9 hours, 15 minutes, including chilling

Apple Pie Filling

4 cups thin, peeled apple wedges
   from a crisp apple (Honeycrisp,
   Ambrosia, Fuji)

½ cup white sugar

2 Tbsp cornstarch

1 cup apple juice

1 Tbsp lemon juice

1 tsp ground cinnamon

½ tsp ground nutmeg

Bread Pudding

1 large loaf (454 g) day-old French
   bread, cut into 1-inch cubes

3 cups whole milk

8 eggs, beaten

⅓ cup white sugar

1 tsp vanilla extract

1 tsp ground cinnamon

¼ tsp ground cloves

¼ tsp ground nutmeg

Streusel Topping

1 cup packed brown sugar

¾ cup rolled oats

¾ cup all-purpose flour

½ cup salted butter

1. To make the filling, place all the apple filling ingredients in a medium-sized sauce pan. Stir until the cornstarch has dissolved, then place on the stove and bring to a low simmer over medium heat, stirring frequently. Cook until the apples are soft and the sauce has thickened and will coat the back of a spoon, 8 to 10 minutes. Remove from the heat and cool in the saucepan.

2. To make the pudding, butter a 9- × 13-inch baking dish (or a casserole of an equivalent capacity). Place the bread cubes in the dish, spreading them out evenly.

3. In a medium-sized bowl, whisk together the milk, eggs, sugar, vanilla, cinnamon, cloves, and nutmeg. Pour the mixture over the bread cubes, ensuring the bread is soaked evenly. Press down on the soaked bread to make an even layer in the bottom of the dish. Spread the apple filling over the bread in an even layer.

4. To make the streusel topping, place the streusel ingredients in a small bowl and mix until crumbly. Spread over the top of the apple filling in an even layer.

5. Cover with plastic wrap and refrigerate for 8 hours or overnight.

6. When ready to bake, preheat the oven to 350°F. Bake for 35 to 40 minutes or until the center of the pudding is set and cooked completely.

7. Remove, cool slightly, and slice. Top with maple syrup or your favorite table syrup.

8. This can be stored in an airtight container in the refrigerator for 2 to 3 days.

Watergate Salad Trifle

Ha! I managed to sneak pistachio pudding into this cookbook twice! This is probably my favorite trifle ever, thanks to my beloved pistachio pudding. Why Watergate Salad is thus named is an unclear part of the dessert's history. It is said that when the recipe was published in a Chicago newspaper, the author renamed it "Watergate" to grab people's attention, as the political scandal was in the headlines at the time. Whatever the case may be, it's one of the most famous dessert salads out there and I wanted to turn it into a trifle. If you are in a hurry, feel free to make the yellow cake from a cake mix. But please do try the homemade yellow cake in this recipe at some point, as it is honestly to die for.

Makes 15–17 servings | Prep Time: 40 minutes | Total Time: 8 hours, 40 minutes

YELLOW CAKE

½ cup butter, softened

1½ cups white sugar

2 eggs + 1 egg yolk

1¼ cups whole milk

1 Tbsp vegetable oil

1 Tbsp vanilla extract

2¼ cups all-purpose flour

2 Tbsp cornstarch

3½ tsp baking powder

1 tsp salt

WATERGATE SALAD

1 cup whipping cream

1 Tbsp white sugar

1 tsp vanilla extract

1 box (3.4 oz/99 g) instant pistachio pudding

1 can (20 oz/567 g) crushed pineapple, undrained

1 cup mini marshmallows

Whipped cream and maraschino cherries, for garnish (optional)

1. Preheat the oven to 350°F. Grease and flour a 9- × 13-inch baking dish.

2. To make the cake, in a stand mixer fitted with the paddle attachment, beat the butter with the sugar until light and fluffy. Beat in the eggs and yolk one at a time, incorporating each before adding the next.

3. In a small bowl, combine the milk, oil, and vanilla.

4. In a medium-sized bowl, whisk together the flour, cornstarch, baking powder, and salt, then beat half into the butter mixture. Beat in half of the milk mixture. Repeat with the remaining flour mixture, then with the remaining milk mixture, beating well after each addition until smooth.

5. Pour into the prepared pan. Bake for 25 to 30 minutes or until a cake tester comes out clean. Remove and place the baking dish on a wire rack and let the cake cool in the pan completely.

6. For the salad, in a stand mixer fitted with the paddle attachment, place the whipping cream, sugar, and vanilla and beat on high speed until the cream is whipped and forms soft peaks when you lift the beater, 4 to 5 minutes.

7. In a large bowl, mix together the pistachio pudding and pineapple (including the juices from the can) until the pudding is dissolved. Add the marshmallows and combine thoroughly. Gently fold in the whipped cream.

8. Cut the cake into 1-inch pieces and place a layer on the bottom of a trifle bowl, or if you don't own one, a large mixing bowl. Take a third of the salad and spread on top. Follow with another cake layer, then salad, then a last cake layer, then the remaining salad. Cover with plastic wrap and refrigerate for a minimum of 8 hours. This is best if you can refrigerate it for up to 24 hours.

9. Top with whipped cream and maraschino cherries (if desired) before serving.

10. This can be stored in the fridge wrapped with plastic wrap for up to 2 days.

Prairie Cherry Black Forest Trifle

There is ***nothing*** like using the sour cherries that grow here on the Prairies for baking and cooking. I love this recipe as it uses three varieties of dwarf sour cherry bushes—Valentine, Cupid, and Juliet—from the University of Saskatchewan that are planted in our front yard. Thanks to the incredible flavor from these sour cherries, you don't need any fake cherry extract at all. If you want a more traditional, slightly boozy Black Forest taste and aren't serving to kids, simply sprinkle 2 tablespoons of kirsch over each layer of cake before adding the cherry layer.

Makes 15–17 servings | Prep Time: 40 minutes | Total Time: 8 hours, 40 minutes

Sour Cherry Filling

4 cups fresh sour cherries, pitted

1 cup white sugar

3 Tbsp cornstarch

Chocolate Trifle Cake

2 cups all-purpose flour

1½ cups white sugar

½ cup Dutch process cocoa powder

1½ tsp baking soda

¾ tsp salt

1½ cups water

¾ cup vegetable oil

1½ tsp vanilla extract

1½ tsp white vinegar

Whipped Cream Layer

3 cups whipping cream

¼ cup white sugar

2 tsp vanilla extract

1. To make the cherry filling, mix together all the filling ingredients in a medium saucepan. Cook over medium heat, stirring occasionally, until the cherries soften and the juices thicken just enough to coat the back of a spoon, 10 to 12 minutes. Remove from the heat and let cool completely.

2. Preheat the oven to 350°F.

3. To make the cake, mix all the cake ingredients together in a large bowl until the batter is smooth. Pour into an ungreased 9- × 13-inch baking pan.

4. Bake for 35 to 40 minutes, until a cake tester inserted in the center comes out clean. Cool in the pan.

5. To make the whipped cream layer, in a stand mixer fitted with the whisk attachment, place the whipping cream, sugar, and vanilla. Beat until light and fluffy, and the cream forms soft peaks when you lift the whisk, 4 to 5 minutes.

6. Cut the cake into roughly 1-inch cubes. Crumble 1 or 2 cubes into smaller crumbs to top the trifle later. Place the rest of the cake cubes in the bottom of a trifle bowl, or if you don't own one, a large mixing bowl. Place a third of the cherry filling on top, followed by a third of the whipped cream. Repeat for another 2 layers, ending with whipped cream.

7. Sprinkle the top layer of whipped cream with the reserved cake crumbs. Cover with plastic wrap and refrigerate overnight for a minimum of 8 hours. This is best if you can refrigerate for up to 24 hours.

8. This can be stored in the fridge wrapped with plastic wrap for up to 2 days.

Ambrosia Salad Squares

I took one of my favorite retro salads and turned it into squares! This dessert slices better than you would expect and serves up perfectly. It's also a gorgeous eye-candy dessert to take with you to parties and picnics. This should be kept chilled until serving, so if you take it outside, make sure you have a cooler! If you want to speed up the process—or simply like using whipped topping—you can substitute 4 cups of whipped topping for the whipped cream.

Makes 15–20 servings | Prep Time: 20 minutes | Total Time: 8 hours, 20 minutes

CRUST

2 cups graham cracker crumbs

½ cup melted salted butter

¼ cup white sugar

FILLING

2 cups whipping cream

2 tsp white sugar

1 tsp vanilla extract

4 cups mini marshmallows, colored or white

1 cup sweetened shredded coconut

1 can (14 fl oz/398 mL) crushed pineapple or pineapple chunks, well drained

TOPPING

2 cans (10 oz/284 mL) mandarin orange segments, drained well

15–20 maraschino cherries, sliced in half

1. Preheat the oven to 350°F.

2. For the crust, place all of the ingredients in a bowl and mix together. Press into the bottom of a 9- × 13-inch baking dish. Bake for 8 to 10 minutes until browned, then remove and cool completely.

3. For the filling, in a stand mixer fitted with the whisk attachment, place the whipping cream, sugar, and vanilla. Whisk until light and fluffy, and the cream forms soft peaks when you lift the whisk, 4 to 5 minutes. Stir in the marshmallows, coconut, and pineapple.

4. Spread the filling over the cooled graham crust.

5. For the topping, place the oranges and cherries on top of the whipping cream layer, creating whatever pattern you like. Press them into the mixture slightly.

6. Cover with plastic wrap and refrigerate overnight. Slice in the pan immediately before serving.

No-Bake Strawberry Ice Cream Cheesecake

If we could use emojis in cookbooks, this frozen cheesecake would rate a fist bump symbol. This cake is meant to be eaten frozen, not at room temperature.

8–10 servings | Prep Time: 20 minutes | Total Time: 8 hours, 45 minutes

Chocolate Crust

2 cups chocolate cookie crumbs

½ cup melted salted butter

1 Tbsp white sugar

Strawberry Sauce

1 cup washed, hulled, and sliced fresh strawberries

¼ cup white sugar

1.25 ounce envelope unflavored gelatin

½ tsp vanilla extract

Cheesecake

2 packages (8 oz/226 g each) cream cheese, softened

1 Tbsp lemon juice

2 cups whipping cream

½ cup white sugar

Chocolate Shell

1¼ cups semi-sweet chocolate chips

3 Tbsp coconut oil

Salted peanuts, halved, for topping

1. To make the crust, place the crust ingredients in a medium bowl and stir well to mix the butter throughout. Press firmly into the bottom of a 9-inch springform pan. Refrigerate for 30 minutes while preparing the other ingredients.

2. To make the sauce, combine the strawberries and sugar in a medium-sized saucepan over medium heat. Cook until the strawberries are soft, breaking them into small pieces with a wooden spoon as you stir, 8 to 10 minutes.

3. Sprinkle the gelatin over 2 tablespoons of tap-cold water, let it sit for 2 minutes, then stir into the strawberries. Continue to cook, stirring until the gelatin has dissolved, 2 to 3 minutes. Remove from the heat and stir in the vanilla. Place the mixture in a bowl and cover with plastic wrap, then place in the refrigerator to cool completely.

4. To make the cheesecake, soften the cream cheese by heating it in 10-second increments in the microwave until it is very soft. Beat together the cream cheese and lemon juice in a medium bowl until creamy and soft.

5. In another medium bowl, add the whipping cream and beat with a handheld mixer until soft peaks form. Add the sugar and continue to beat until thick, 2 to 3 minutes. Gently fold the cream cheese mixture into the whipping cream until combined. Fold in the strawberry sauce. Spoon the mixture onto the chilled crust. Cover with plastic wrap and freeze for 8 hours or overnight.

6. To serve, remove the sides of the springform pan and leave the cake on the bottom piece. Melt the chocolate chips and coconut oil together in the microwave or in a bain-marie, then pour over the cold cake. Sprinkle with the salted peanuts immediately before the chocolate sets.

7. Let the cake warm up at room temperature for 15 to 20 minutes (until you can just slice it!), then use a hot knife to cut through the chocolate shell and still-frozen cake. Alternatively, to make it easier to serve, you can pour the hard shell onto each individual piece after you cut the slices, then sprinkle with peanuts.

8. To store, place the springform pan ring back on, wrap the cake in plastic wrap, and return it to the freezer. Just don't let it melt too much before doing so.

Chocolate Pumpkin Lasagna

cheater!

Pumpkin and chocolate are one of the most delicious pairings ever—and when you throw in some pumpkin pie spice? Perfection! This recipe may have a lot of ingredients, but it's super easy to prepare. I also cheat by using chocolate pudding to make life a little easier. Desserts that have many layers to them are now often called "lasagnas," a modern name for what is basically a dessert slice—except don't expect it to slice perfectly! They can be a little messy, but who needs perfection when something tastes this good?

Makes 10–12 servings | Prep Time: 30 minutes | Total Time: 1 day, 30 minutes

COOKIE CRUST

25 chocolate cookies with a cream filling

½ cup chocolate cookie crumbs

½ cup melted salted butter

WHIPPED CREAM MIXTURE

2½ cups whipping cream

3 Tbsp white sugar

1 tsp pumpkin pie spice

½ tsp vanilla extract

CREAM CHEESE LAYER

1 package (8 oz/226 g) cream cheese, softened

1 cup icing sugar

PUMPKIN LAYER

2½ cups milk

2 packages (4 oz/113 g each) instant chocolate pudding mix

1 can (19 fl oz/540 mL) pumpkin pie filling

1½ tsp pumpkin pie spice

1. To make the crust, place the cookies in a food processor and pulse until you have crumbs. Pour into a bowl. Add the chocolate cookie crumbs (at this point, set aside some of the crumbs mixture for the topping, if desired) and melted butter and stir until the crumbs are all moistened. Press into the bottom of a 9- × 13-inch baking pan.

2. To make the whipped cream mixture, place the whipping cream, sugar, pumpkin pie spice, and vanilla in a stand mixer fitted with the whisk attachment. Whisk the mixture on high speed until the cream is whipped and soft peaks form. Set aside.

3. To make the cream cheese layer, in another large bowl, combine the cream cheese and icing sugar. Using a hand mixer to beat until completely smooth and creamy. Fold in 1 cup of the whipping cream mixture. Spread this onto the chocolate crust in an even layer.

4. To make the pumpkin layer, combine the milk and chocolate pudding mix in a large bowl and, using a hand mixer, beat for 2 minutes until smooth. Add the pumpkin pie filling and spice, and mix thoroughly. Fold in 1 cup of the whipped cream mixture, and then spread the mixture in an even layer on top of the cream cheese layer.

5. Spread the rest of the whipped cream mixture on top, and sprinkle with cookie crumbs if desired. Cover with plastic wrap and refrigerate for 8 hours or overnight. Serve cold.

6. This will last wrapped up in the fridge for up to 2 days but is best eaten right away.

Coconut Strawberry Rhubarb Oatmeal Bake

While I would call this dessert a fruit crisp in spirit, the version that my family makes has egg in the topping, which turns it into a cakey, dense topping that soaks up the juices perfectly. Picture a layer of dense, nutty-textured oatmeal-coconut cake on top of the fruit layer. It's not quite a crisp and not quite a fruit cobbler; it's somewhere in between, so I've called it a bake! Another lovely thing about this recipe is that it's a two-for-one deal—omit the egg and you have a classic fruit crisp topping that will crunch up while baking. The choice is up to you!

Makes 12–14 servings | Prep Time: 20 minutes | Total Time: 1 hour to 1 hour, 10 minutes

Filling

10 cups ⅓-inch-thick rhubarb pieces

4 cups sliced strawberries

1¼ cups white sugar

½ cup packed brown sugar

⅓ cup cornstarch

Topping

2 cups all-purpose flour

2 cups packed brown sugar

1 cup rolled oats

1 cup sweetened shredded coconut

2 eggs, well beaten (omit if you are making a crisp instead of a bake)

1 cup melted salted butter

◆ ◆ ◆

I make my filling a tad bit sour to provide a contrast to the very sweet, rich topping. You can add another ¼ cup white sugar if you like a sweeter filling.

◆ ◆ ◆

1. Preheat the oven to 350°F. Grease a 9- × 13-inch baking dish.
2. To make the filling, in a large bowl, place all of the filling ingredients. Toss them together to coat the fruit evenly. Spoon into the prepared baking dish and spread out in an even layer.
3. To make the topping, in a medium bowl, mix the topping ingredients until they form a thick, slightly tacky dough. Drop dollops of dough on top of the fruit filling until the fruit is mostly covered. (If you wish to make a crisp, omit the eggs and combine the rest of the topping ingredients by hand until crumbly, then sprinkle over the top of the fruit evenly, covering as much of the fruit as you can.)
4. Bake for 40 to 50 minutes, until the top is browned and the fruit has been bubbling for at least 5 minutes. Remove and cool until you can safely serve it warm.
5. Top with vanilla ice cream and enjoy.
6. This is best eaten the day you bake it, but after baking it will last in your fridge for up to 3 days, or in your freezer for up to 3 months. Simply cover the pan with plastic wrap and aluminum foil, and freeze. To warm from frozen, reheat in a 300°F oven until heated through.

Chapter Eight

LIBATIONS

▼▲▼▲▼▲▼▲▼▲▼▲▼▲▼

THE PRAIRIE BARTENDER

BY MR. KITCHEN MAGPIE

And now, by popular demand, here is my husband, creator of cocktails and mocktails, and home bartender extraordinaire: Mr. Kitchen Magpie.

Our home bar came about because something inside of me died a little bit every time I saw the ever-rising prices on modern cocktail menus. Some call it being cheap; I call it my frugal Scottish genes. The other half of me is Irish, which leaves me with a love of whiskey, a trait that could easily rack up a hefty bar tab. By the time you add up the cost of a taxi and a couple of cocktails at $15 apiece (which seems to be the norm nowadays), you can easily end up paying well over $100 for an evening out for two—and that's just the pre-dinner warm-up. When you entertain at home, however, that same amount of money translates into a couple of bottles of your favorite spirits, which you can use to make numerous cocktails. Yes, it's fun to go out every now and again, but I also take so much joy in entertaining at our home bar. Why? Because there's something incredibly satisfying about being able to put together your favorite cocktails and entertaining guests in the comfort of your own home.

My love of mixology made me the obvious choice for the role of Prairie bartender during our Big Ukrainian Party on the Prairie. During the hustle and bustle of preparations for hosting 30-plus relatives out at the family farm, Karlynn's dad turned to me and said, "Mike, I'm putting you in charge of the drinks." Done and done! Having met a couple of Karlynn's uncles and cousins, I already knew that they were scotch drinkers. I brought my traveling bar case, some of my favorite vintage roly-poly glasses and some scotch for them to try, as you can see in the photo on the previous page.

Since there were children ranging from age 2 to 14, all of whom were going to be running around on a hot sunny day out at the farm, I knew that I need something sparkling water–based for hydration, sweet with juice, and large in volume so that I didn't have to keep replacing it. It also needed to be delicious enough to appeal to the nondrinkers in the family. Thus my Family-Friendly Sangria Punch (page 245) was born, but despite my preparation, I had to refill it four or five times thanks to its popularity with all of the guests. For the adults, I made a classic cocktail in the form of several pitchers of Long Island Iced Tea (page 248), multiplying that single-serving recipe many times over to make sure Karlynn's relatives never had an empty glass. It was also the perfect opportunity to get in one last taste-test of Mr. Kitchen Magpie's Gin and Juice (page 233) before deeming it cookbook worthy.

The key to a successful home bar is having the right ingredients and spirits on hand so you have what feels like unlimited choices for you and your guests. On pages 224–25, you'll find some tips on stocking your home bar with all the drinks, mixers, and accessories you're likely going to ever need.

A great home bar is also in the decor. I'm not saying you need anything fancy—we found our furnishings, including a blue retro sectional couch, at our local thrift store one Friday morning—just comforting. We then continued the retro theme with vintage barware, old board games, and an amazing pinball machine (thanks to Karlynn's dad).

The retro theme fits our family, but whatever theme or style you choose to go with, the experience of watching everything come together is priceless. Our home bar is now one of my favorite places to be in the house (and not just because of the readily available alcohol), and no matter how many times I stop to look at it, it still makes me smile. If you have your own bar, feel free to reach out to us through our social media (see the back cover of this book): there's nothing we love more than bar pictures!

—Mike (aka Mr. Kitchen Magpie)

◆ ◆ ◆

Yields Tip

All the high-yield cocktail recipes I have presented in this chapter can be easily scaled down with simple division for one or two servings. Better yet, use your mad multiplication skills and multiply them by two, magically turning the drink from four servings into eight. Now that's my kind of math!

◆ ◆ ◆

STOCKING YOUR HOME BAR

After years of stocking my own home bar (and seeing what I use most), I have gathered my ultimate list of bar tools, perishables, liquors and pantry items. Of course, you'll want to make sure you have plenty of ice as well. While not all the items listed here are required unless you are planning to try every drink within this chapter (you've gotta have goals!), it should give you a general idea of what you may need when stocking a home bar.

LIQUOR CABINET

Bitters

Angostura bitters

Fee Brothers Old Fashion Aromatic Bitters

Brandy

Gin

Sloe gin

Liqueurs

Amaretto

Baileys Irish Cream

Cabot Trail Maple Cream or equivalent

Chambord

Cointreau

Grand Marnier

Kahlúa

Triple sec

Rum

Jamaican rum

White rum

Tequila

Gold tequila

Silver tequila

Whiskey

Canadian Club or equivalent whiskey

Cherry whiskey

Wine

Red

Sparkling pink Moscato

Vodka

BAR TOOLS

Beer bottle opener

Boston shaker

Cheese cloth

Corkscrew

Cocktail sticks

Ice bucket

Long-handled bar spoon

Mold for large ice cubes

Muddler

GLASSWARE

Brandy glasses

Champagne flutes

Highball glasses

Hurricane glasses

Roly-polys

Shot glasses

Tall tumblers

Tom Collins glasses

Whiskey tumblers

Wine glasses

PANTRY

Cinnamon sticks

Ground coffee

Honey

Lapsang souchong tea

Pineapple chunks (canned)

Sugar

Brown sugar

White sugar

PERISHABLES

Creams

Vanilla ice cream

Whipping cream

Herbs

Fresh basil

Fresh mint

Fresh rosemary

Juice

Grape juice (purple)

Lemon juice

Lemonade

Lime juice

Orange juice

Pineapple juice

Produce

Apples

Cranberries (fresh or frozen)

Egg whites (pasteurized in the carton)

English cucumber

Lemons

Limes

Maraschino cherries

Oranges

Rhubarb (fresh or frozen)

Strawberries (frozen)

SODA

Club soda (plain; lemon/lime
    flavored are also fine)

Cola

Sparkling water

SYRUP

Grenadine

Lime cordial

Maple (pure is best)

Simple syrups (see pages 228–30)

How to Make Cold-Brewed vs. Iced Coffee

Life-skills alert! As someone who works from home when his children are off school during the summer, I have found a new best friend in iced coffee during the hot months. However, did you know that there are two ways of making it? Technically I'm wrong in referring to all cold coffee as "iced coffee," as there are two types: cold-brewed coffee and actual iced coffee. Each one has its own distinct taste and requires different techniques to make it. Try them both and decide which one you prefer.

Note: I don't kid around with my coffee. I love a good, strong coffee, and these coffees are stronger than most recipes out there. These are meant to be enjoyed with cream and sugar, so if you don't take these in your hot coffee, add extra ice cubes to your cold coffee to dilute it—it will result in the most delicious beverage!

Double note: The best thing you can do for yourself coffee-wise is to buy a glass drip brew coffee carafe with the cone drip filter that attaches to the top. Drip coffee made with a cone filter simply tastes better.

Triple note: If you bring this to a party, you will be the most loved person there. Especially if you happen to sneak some Baileys along with you. Better make a double batch. —*Mr K.M.*

ICED COFFEE

Iced coffee is coffee that you brew hot, then cool down with ice cubes. Connoisseurs claim that using hot water is the best way to capture all the taste benefits of coffee.

Makes 7–8 cups of coffee | Prep Time: 15 minutes |
Cooling Time: 5 minutes (or until ice has melted) | Total Time: 20 minutes

2 cups ground coffee

5 cups boiling water

2 cups ice cubes (3 cups for weaker coffee)

1. Place the ground coffee in the top part of a drip-brew coffee carafe with a cone filter top attached, with a filter placed inside. Pour the 5 cups of hot water over the coffee, letting it drip through the filter. Alternatively, you can prepare your coffee in your coffee maker using the above amounts.

2. Place all of the ice cubes in a large lidded heat-safe glass jug and pour the hot, freshly brewed coffee over top. Add more ice (if desired) until the coffee reaches the desired strength.

3. Wait until the ice has melted and then serve cold, with cream and sugar and additional ice if desired. Store in the fridge until using. It should keep for up to 2 weeks, but the flavor will begin to degrade if you keep it longer than a week.

COLD-BREWED COFFEE

Cold-brewed coffee takes some time and preparation, but it's my favorite way of making cold coffee in the summer months. It is less acidic than its hot-brewed counterpart.

Makes 8 cups of coffee | Prep Time: 5 minutes |
Cooling Time: 8 hours | Total Time: 8 hours, 5 minutes

8 cups cold water

4 cups ground coffee

1. Place the water and ground coffee in a large pitcher and cover with plastic wrap. Let sit overnight in the fridge.

2. The next morning, strain the coffee through the cone of your drip-brew coffee maker fitted with a filter. Alternatively, you can use cheesecloth doubled over many times, but the cone is easier by far. Filter, then transfer to a lidded pitcher in the fridge. This should keep for up to 2 weeks, but the flavor will begin to degrade after 1 week. Use as a coffee concentrate, adding ice cubes, cream, and sugar to taste.

Simple Syrups

Simple syrup is a staple in any home bartender's repertoire and, thankfully, it's also incredibly easy to make. In cocktail books from the 1960s and earlier, you'll often find that the recipes call for confectioner's sugar (otherwise known as icing sugar). That was how some bartenders sweetened their drinks before simple syrup became so commonplace. And thank goodness for simple syrup, since it results in a tastier drink. The switch to simple syrup was made for a number of reasons: it adds volume to drinks, resulting in less alcohol being used and reduced costs, it's not a messy powder, and it's far more concentrated than sugar on its own.

Some recipes out there suggest making simple syrup with a 1:1 sugar-to-water ratio. This tastes just fine, but it will only last about 2 weeks. When you use a 2:1 sugar-to-water ratio, however, the simple syrup lasts up to 6 months because of the higher sugar content. —*Mr K.M.*

The yields for all the simple syrup recipes in this chapter are approximate. They vary according to how long you boil the mixture and how juicy the berries are in the fruit syrups. Treat all yields as very flexible and remember that when you combine 1 cup of sugar with 1 cup of water, you are not getting 2 cups of syrup, as the sugar dissolves.

❖ ❖ ❖

TRADITIONAL SIMPLE SYRUP

While you can buy simple syrups in the store, I can't think of a good reason why you should. Making your own at home is easy and cheap, and with my flavor customizations below, you will have a simple syrup arsenal at the ready for cocktail and mocktail crafting.

Makes about 2 cups | Prep Time: 10 minutes |
Cooling Time: 2 hours | Total Time: 2 hours, 15 minutes

1 cup water

2 cups white sugar

1. Place the water in a saucepan over medium heat and bring to a slow boil. Add the sugar and stir until dissolved. Remove from the heat once all of the sugar has dissolved and let cool. Store in a sealed glass jar in the fridge.

VARIATIONS:

Rosemary Add 2 sprigs of fresh rosemary once sugar is dissolved and let simmer for 3 to 5 minutes, stirring occasionally. Let cool, strain, and store.

Basil Add 10 to 15 fresh basil leaves once the sugar is dissolved and muddle to release the oils. Let simmer for 3 to 5 minutes, stirring occasionally. Let cool, strain, and store.

Mint Add 15 to 20 mint leaves once the sugar is dissolved and muddle to release the oils. Let simmer for 3 to 5 minutes, stirring occasionally. Let cool, strain, and store.

BROWN SUGAR SIMPLE SYRUP

While most simple syrup is made with white sugar, that doesn't mean it's the only option. Brown sugar simple syrup pairs very well with rum-based cocktails thanks to its richness. You wouldn't want to use it in gin- or vodka-based cocktails given its color, but it works perfectly for drinks that have amber spirits, such as my Mr. Kitchen Magpie's Old-Fashioned (see page 251) or drinks with colas, like my Long Island Iced Tea on page 248.

Makes about 2 cups | Prep Time: 5 minutes |
Cooling Time: 2 hours | Total Time: 2 hours, 5 minutes

1 cup water

1⅓ cup brown sugar

1. In a saucepan, bring the water to a slow boil over medium heat.
2. Add the brown sugar and stir until dissolved.
3. Remove from heat and let cool.
4. Store in a mason jar or similar airtight glass container in the fridge for up to 2 weeks.

STRAWBERRY RHUBARB SIMPLE SYRUP

Perfect for summer—and Strawberry Rhubarb Gin Fizz (see page 238)—this simple syrup is a great way to use up the rhubarb from your garden.

Makes about 4 cups | Prep Time: 10 minutes |
Cooling Time: 2 hours | Total Time: 2 hours, 10 minutes

2 cups water

2 cups white sugar

4 cups chopped rhubarb (fresh or frozen)

2 cups chopped frozen strawberries

1. Place the water in a saucepan over medium heat and bring to a slow boil. Add the sugar and stir until dissolved. Add the rhubarb and strawberries and simmer for 3 to 5 minutes, stirring occasionally. Remove from the heat and let cool.

2. Strain into a sealed glass jar and store in the fridge for up to 2 weeks.

SMOKY SIMPLE SYRUP

This is my favorite simple syrup. I came up with this because I wanted a simple syrup that added a smoky flavor to my cocktails—particularly my Mr. Kitchen Magpie's Old-Fashioned (page 251). Lapsang souchong is an excellent tea that has a distinct smoky flavor. It's perfect for this because you can increase or decrease the amount of smoke flavor you want simply by adding or removing tea bags.

Makes about 2 cups | Prep Time: 5 minutes |
Cooling Time: 2 hours | Total Time: 2 hours, 5 minutes

1 cup water

3–4 bags of lapsang souchong tea

2 cups white sugar

1. In a medium saucepan, bring the water to a boil. Once boiled, remove from heat and add 3 to 4 tea bags. Let the tea steep for about 5 minutes.

2. Remove the tea bags and return the saucepan to the stove. Bring to a slow boil over medium heat and add the sugar, stirring until dissolved. Remove from the heat and let cool.

3. Store in a sealed glass jar in the fridge for up to 6 weeks.

Homemade Sweet and Sour Mix

With my love of whiskey and amaretto sours, it just makes sense to always have some sweet and sour mix readily available. I keep a large mason jar of this in the door of the fridge, and with the recipe below, you can easily get several months out of it before it's time to make a fresh batch, thanks to the addition of the citrus. This recipe is great because you can scale it up or down quite easily. I use this primarily in my Amaretto Sour on page 241. —Mr K.M.

Makes about 2½ cups | Prep Time: 10 minutes |
Cooling Time: 2 hours | Total Time: 2 hours, 10 minutes

1 cup water

2 cups white sugar

1 cup lemon juice (4 large lemons)

½ cup lime juice (about 4 medium limes)

1. Bring the water to a boil over medium heat.
2. Add the sugar and stir until it is dissolved. Remove from the heat.
3. Pour the simple syrup into a sealed glass jar and let cool in the fridge.
4. Once the simple syrup has cooled (about 2 hours), it's time to add the lemon and lime juice. If your lemon juice has pulp in it, strain it into the simple syrup and discard the pulp. Now add the lime juice. Put the lid on the container and shake vigorously to combine.
5. This mixture should last in the fridge for up to 6 months. It will become cloudy when it's close to expiration, indicating that it's time to make a fresh batch.

Mike's Gin and Juice

My gin and juice recipe came about because Karlynn and I wanted to take something with us to a friend's house for a party. I looked toward the fruit bowl for inspiration, and true to form, the kids had eaten everything BUT the oranges and lemons. (What, they don't like lemons for school lunches?) It was then that we discovered the taste combination that is basil simple syrup and gin, so the logical next step was to throw it all together and see what happened. You can add fresh basil leaves to this if you want to add extra color, but since we aren't big fans of our straws getting clogged with leaves, we chose to leave them whole and use our basil simple syrup for the flavoring instead. This recipe halves easily. —Mr K.M.

Makes one 8–10 cup pitcher | Prep Time: 10 minutes | Total Time: 10 minutes

2 cups gin

¾ cup triple sec

1½ cups fresh lemon juice (about 6 large lemons)

½ cup orange juice (2 to 3 oranges)

1–1½ cups Basil Simple Syrup (page 229)

1 orange

1 lemon

6–8 fresh basil leaves, for garnish and color (optional)

1. Place the gin, triple sec, lemon juice, orange juice, and basil simple syrup in an 8- to 10-cup clear glass pitcher. Stir well.

2. Thinly slice 1 orange and 1 lemon crosswise and add them to the pitcher. Add the fresh basil leaves for color if desired. (We use basil simple syrup for the flavor, so excluding them will not change the flavor.)

❖ ❖ ❖

The best way to use up citrus fruits that are close to expiration is to turn them into juice for cocktails, at least in our house. You can also get away with cutting up slightly dried-out lemons, oranges, or limes and putting them into your cocktails to rehydrate and add color. Of course, you'll want to make sure you are putting them into similarly flavored cocktails.

❖ ❖ ❖

Sparkling Gin Gimlet

Ever since we had our *Mad Men* party, the Gin Gimlet has been a popular drink whenever we have people over. A much-requested cocktail in the 1950s and '60s, the Gin Gimlet is a deceptively strong drink. For this reason, when you want the taste of one but want to water it down a bit, the Sparkling Gin Gimlet is a great option. My son, Kade, is a big lover of club soda, so we tend to buy it in many flavors, which led me to wonder how well lemon club soda would work in a standard Gin Gimlet. The result is this cocktail. —*Mr K.M.*

Makes 1 cocktail | Prep Time: 5 minutes | Total Time: 5 minutes

2½ oz gin

1 oz Rose's Lime Cordial

½ oz fresh lime juice

2 oz plain club soda (lemon/lime flavor is also fine)

Ice cubes (enough for the shaker + glass)

1 slice of lime, for garnish (optional)

1. Place the gin, lime cordial, and lime juice in a Boston shaker with 2 to 3 ice cubes. Shake until the metal is cold to the touch.

2. Pour over 3 to 4 ice cubes in a tumbler or Tom Collins glass. Add the club soda and stir briefly so as not to flatten the club soda.

3. Garnish with lime, if desired.

VARIATIONS WITHOUT CLUB SODA:

1. *Traditional gimlet:* after step 1, pour drink into a martini glass.
2. *The Bennett:* add 2 dashes Angostura Bitters to step 1.
3. *The Stay Up Late:* add 1 oz cognac to step 1.
4. *The Debutante:* add 2 tsps grenadine and 1 dash Angostura Bitters to step 1.

GREAT DANE

Nicole's Gin Basil Smash

"Hey, Nicole," Karlynn said between the final sips of her second gin smash cocktail in 45 minutes, "what exactly is in these drinks?"

"Hey, Duane!" Nicole yelled to her husband, who was manning the barbecue. "What's in these gin smashes?"

Duane came in, wiped his hands clean from the barbecue, and said: "Lemon juice, simple syrup, and four shots of gin."

If you are a fan of the cocktails section of the Kitchen Magpie website, you may be familiar with this story, as Nicole's gin basil smash was one of the first cocktail recipes on there. These are dangerously delicious drinks, so make sure you warn your guests! You can only make one at a time—which is probably a very, very good thing. —*Mr K.M.*

Makes 1 cocktail | Prep Time: 5 minutes | Total Time: 5 minutes

2 oz Basil Simple Syrup (page 229)

2 oz lemon juice

4 oz gin

Ice cubes (enough for the shaker + glass)

8–10 leaves fresh basil, for garnish (optional)

1. Place the basil simple syrup and lemon juice in a cocktail shaker.
2. Pour in the gin and then add ice cubes. Put the lid on the shaker and shake until the shaker is freezing cold to the touch.
3. Pour into a tumbler or Tom Collins glass and add enough ice to fill the glass.
4. Add basil leaves if desired for color.

Strawberry Rhubarb Gin Fizz

Rhubarb makes a great addition to cocktails and simple syrups, and this drink is no exception. This drink will require the Strawberry Rhubarb Simple Syrup on page 230. This recipe makes one sweet and summery pitcher, making it a perfect drink for sipping on the deck in the hot sun. This is Karlynn's favorite summer cocktail. —Mr K.M.

Makes one 8–10 cup pitcher | Prep Time: 10 minutes | Total Time: 10 minutes

1½ cups gin

1½ cups Strawberry Rhubarb Simple Syrup (page 230)

1 oz lemon juice

Ice cubes

1 bottle (750 mL) sparkling pink Moscato

1 lemon, sliced thinly

Rhubarb stalks, for garnish

1. Place the gin, simple syrup, and lemon juice in a pitcher filled about one-third with ice.
2. Pour in the Moscato and then add the lemon slices. Stir with a long-handled bar spoon and let cool for about 5 minutes before serving.
3. Garnish with rhubarb stalks.

Amaretto Sour

Many years ago, when I was just barely past the legal drinking age, a friend and I decided that it would be a good idea to sneak into his parents' liquor cabinet for something to drink. The only thing in it was a bottle of amaretto, which we proceeded to polish off between the two of us. In my naïveté, I did not know the benefits of knowing when enough is enough, and as such suffered greatly the next morning (and in fact the entire next day). Ever since, even the smell of amaretto made my stomach turn. That was, however, until recently when I rediscovered the beauty of this spirit when enjoyed *in moderation*. I'm a huge fan of sours, and this was the first thing I made with amaretto since that day many years ago. —*Mr K.M.*

Makes 1 cocktail | Prep Time: 5 minutes | Total Time: 5 minutes

1½ oz amaretto

¾ oz bourbon

1 oz lemon juice

½ oz egg white, beaten (optional)

1 tsp Traditional Simple Syrup (page 229)

2 to 3 dashes of Angostura bitters

Ice cubes (enough for the shaker + glass)

1. Place all of the ingredients in a Boston shaker with ice and shake until the shaker is cold to the touch.
2. Pour over ice in a whiskey tumbler or in a roly-poly, with 1 or 2 ice cubes.

VARIATIONS:

Amaretto Shore Sour: add a splash of orange juice.

Amaretto Vodka Sour: swap the bourbon for vodka.

Maple Mudslide

Here is a great Canadian-themed cocktail that is basically like drinking dessert. What could be more Canadian than a maple-flavored cocktail? I only recently discovered maple cream liqueur, and it's a great variation on the traditional mudslide. —*Mr K.M.*

Makes 1 cocktail | Prep Time: 5 minutes | Total Time: 5 minutes

1 oz vodka

1 oz Kahlúa

1 oz maple cream liqueur

1 scoop vanilla ice cream

1 cup ice cubes

Whipped cream, for garnish

Maple syrup, for garnish

1. Place the vodka, Kahlúa, maple cream liqueur, ice cream, and ice in a blender. Blend until smooth.
2. Pour into a hurricane glass and top with whipped cream and maple syrup.

Russian Cucumber Lemonade

Karlynn decided that this vodka-based cocktail had to be called Russian Cucumber Lemonade to honor her Russian roots. These amounts are for an 8-cup pitcher's worth, so this is perfect if you have guests or relatives. Cucumber and mint make an amazing combination, but the lemonade takes this to a whole new level. —*Mr K.M.*

Makes one 8-cup pitcher | Prep Time: 5 minutes | Total Time: 5 minutes

Six ½-inch slices English cucumber (unpeeled), plus extra for garnish

12 mint leaves

12 oz vodka

32 oz lemonade

1. Place the cucumber, mint leaves, and 2 ounces of the vodka in a pitcher and muddle to release the oils in the mint leaves and crush the cucumber.
2. Add the remaining 10 ounces of vodka and then stir in the lemonade.
3. Serve in a Tom Collins glass over ice.

Red Wine Whiskey Sangria

Red Wine Whiskey Sangria

Disclaimer: I'm a big fan of whiskey-based cocktails. Thus, I wanted to try making a sangria with whiskey (because why not?) and this is what I came up with. When you add a sweeter-tasting whiskey like Canadian Club to a fruity wine, the combination might entice those who prefer sweeter drinks to give a whiskey-based libation a try. It gets even better when you pair it with Grand Marnier, which gives it the nice citrus flavor that is essential to this drink. —*Mr K.M.*

Makes one 8-cup pitcher | Prep Time: 5 minutes | Total Time: 5 minutes

2½ cups ice cubes

1 bottle (750 mL) fruity red wine

1 cup Canadian Club whiskey

⅓ cup Grand Marnier

1 orange, cut into thin slices

1. Fill an 8-cup pitcher with the ice cubes. Add the wine, whiskey, Grand Marnier, and orange slices.
2. Give the mixture a stir with a long-handled bar spoon and serve chilled.

Family-Friendly Sangria Punch

Sometimes you want to make a nonalcoholic drink available. This is an excellent option for those who abstain, and while it does take a bit of effort to put together, it's well worth it. The recipe below fills a 24-cup punch bowl. —*Mr K.M.*

Makes one 24-cup punch bowl | Prep Time: 15 minutes |
Total Time: 2 hours, 15 minutes

6 cups purple grape juice

1½ cups apple juice

1½ cups orange juice

¼ cup lemon juice (1 large lemon)

2 cups frozen pineapple chunks

2 oranges, sliced into rounds, with peel

2 apples, cored and sliced into rounds, with peel

6 cups sparkling water (about two 750 mL bottles)

1. Pour all four types of juice into a 24-cup-capacity punch bowl.
2. Add the fruit and stir.
3. Refrigerate for at least 2 to 3 hours.
4. Add the sparkling water right before serving.

Long Island Iced Tea

I made a couple of pitchers of these for our now infamous Big Ukrainian Party on the Prairie, mentioned on page 4, and they were gone just as quickly as I could get them out the door. This recipe makes a single drink, but it doubles, triples, and quadruples easily. I drank these for years until I broadened my horizons and started making my own cocktails, but they're still a favorite of mine. The one thing that surprises most people about them is the sheer number of alcoholic ingredients it takes to make one, but it's worth it. —Mr K.M.

Makes 1 cocktail | Prep Time: 5 minutes | Total Time: 5 minutes

¾ oz gin

¾ oz white rum

¾ oz silver tequila

¾ oz vodka

¾ oz triple sec

¾ oz Traditional Simple Syrup (page 229)

¾ oz lemon juice

Cola

1 lemon, sliced, for garnish

1. Place the gin, rum, tequila, vodka, triple sec, simple syrup, and lemon juice in a Boston shaker with ice and shake until the shaker is cold to the touch.
2. Pour into a tumbler filled with 3 to 4 ice cubes and add a splash of cola. Stir in lemon if desired.
3. Give it a stir with a bar spoon or cocktail stick, adjust to taste, and enjoy!

✦ ✦ ✦

Tip

For a Long Beach Tea, simply switch the cola for cranberry juice.

✦ ✦ ✦

Long Island
Iced Tea

Mr. Kitchen Magpie's Old-Fashioned

The one drink you will find me with most often is not a Long Island Iced Tea (page 248) but an Old-Fashioned. I am, however, very particular about how they are made. After trying many different methods, I've settled on this one as my tried and true method. My love for this drink came about after binge-watching *Mad Men* with Karlynn. This drink is best made with the same whiskey they used in the show: Canadian Club.

Personally, I free-pour this drink, but for the purposes of this book, I've supplied measurements. I'll also add that using any ice other than a large round or square ice cube is a cardinal sin and makes for a far less enjoyable drink. Also, quite a few recipes call for Angostura bitters, but frankly, I find they are not as good as the Old Fashion Aromatic Bitters from Fee Brothers. I refuse to use anything else. —*Mr K.M.*

Makes 1 cocktail | Prep Time: 5 minutes | Total Time: 5 minutes

1 slice orange

1 maraschino cherry

1 Tbsp Traditional Simple Syrup (page 229) or syrup from the maraschino cherry jar

1 large round or square ice cube

2–3 oz Canadian Club whiskey

3 dashes of Fee Brothers Old Fashion Aromatic Bitters

1. Place the orange slice in a whiskey glass and add the cherry and simple syrup. Muddle everything together with a muddler to get the juice out of the orange slice and crush the cherry.
2. Place the ice cube on top and pour the Canadian Club whiskey over it, to taste.
3. Add 3 dashes of the bitters and give everything a slight stir with a spoon to mix the bitters into the drink.

Thank-Yous

A nd here we are with book #2! Even after learning what it's actually like to write and photograph a cookbook (blood, sweat, tears, weight gain—and that right there is why they compare writing a book to having a child!), I still went and did it again—and again, I couldn't have done it alone.

First: you, my readers. Thank you to every single one of you who bought my first cookbook, because if you hadn't, this one wouldn't have come to be. You proved that I wasn't going to bankrupt my publisher with my blogger style of food writing, and that yes indeed, contrary to popular belief, some people actually do like food bloggers. Occasionally. In small doses.

We all need to thank my mom, because she finally let me share our family perogy recipe. She had endless patience even though I lost the copies of recipes she wrote out for me (that potato salad did not want to get published), forgot to write things down, and called her countless times to ask the same thing (because I forgot to write it down; sense a pattern?). And she also helped bring together the Ukrainian chapter. That was the hardest writing I have ever done, when I tried to translate what we just "know" into words to teach it to you.

Thanks to my dad, who spent weeks getting the farm ready for the Big Ukrainian Party on the Prairie. Tents, and lawn care, and chair rentals, oh my!

All of my family members who made it out for the Ukrainian party, what a weekend that was! Thank you cousin Karlee for your party and family photos!

Everyone at Appetite by Random House who worked on this book. Robert McCullough for again having faith in my cookbook concept. Lindsay Paterson and Katherine Stopa, my editors, who had the most difficult job in the world editing my recipes, ramblings, and musings. Designer Leah Springate, who again hit the nail on the head with the design for this book.

If you are a dedicated enough reader to be reading my thank-yous, then I shall reveal the tomato soup cake's mystery woman, L.F., as Liane Faulder. Huge thanks to her for her unwavering support of me in the local Edmonton food scene for nigh on nine years now. She's always ready to come over for a slice of pie and writes the most beautiful newspaper articles about me. Flattery is the key to getting more pie, you know.

Thank you to all my friends who have put up with me hiding away in my house, cooking and writing, missing dinners and events because of deadlines, and generally putting up with how flaky I am while writing a cookbook.

Thank you, Kade and Ivy, for putting up with being the kids of a food blogger. Actually, now you have two food blogger parents with me roping your dad into the biz. Everyone thinks living with a food blogger is all delicious food, but you know better. It's eating lukewarm meals at weird times because my lighting wasn't right or I needed that last video shot. It's getting extra lectures to behave yourselves in public. (Remember that time the cashier recognized you? Keep remembering that. You're both still lucky that you miraculously weren't teenagering all over the place that time.) It's eating toast for dinner because all I did all day was test a cake recipe—three times. Love you, twerps.

And always last but not least, thanks to Mr. Kitchen Magpie (whose real name is Mike) for helping me out with this book and on the website—and providing me with many delicious cocktails during the making of this book. Thanks for holding down the fort when I'm neck-deep in cookbook edits and cranky as all get-out. It takes an amazing husband to encourage his wife to write a second cookbook when he barely survived her mood during edits with the first one. And, as always, thank you for being head dishwasher in the family, as most days I'd rather throw them out than wash them.

Glassware Index

My vintage glassware obsession hasn't stopped since publishing my first cookbook, which featured a taste of the assortment of vintage dishes, platters, casserole dishes and more. As you might have guessed, my collection has grown by leaps and bounds since then, and has now completely taken over the left side of my garage. Mr. Kitchen Magpie has also joined the fray with vintage barware and glasses for his cocktails. Luckily, his collection is comprised of much smaller items so it doesn't take up as much room as mine . . . otherwise we'd be moving to a larger house to accommodate it all!

A disclaimer: I'm not a vintage glassware expert by any means, I'm a collector. So when it comes to the naming of patterns, I search the names on the internet just like everyone else. If there are mistakes in the following pattern names, I apologize in advance!

Pyrex Butterfly Gold & Harvest Display

Pyrex Old Orchard Set

Bartlett Collins Cookie Jars

Luster Cocktail Set

My Mug Door

Hazel Atlas Wheat Bowls

Pyrex Butterprint

My Current Hutch Display

My 1970's Pyrex Display

Trio of Vintage Owls

Pyrex Harvest Fridge Set

Index